MASTER THE BASICS:

ITALIAN

by
Marcel Danesi, Ph.D.
University of Toronto

Barron's Educational Series, Inc.

All inquiries should be addressed to:
Barron's Educational Series, Inc.
250 Wireless Boulevard
Hauppauge, New York 11788

Library of Congress Catalog Card No. 86-26607
International Standard Book No. 0-8120-3771-5

Library of Congress Cataloging-in-Publication Data

Danesi, Marcel, 1946–
  Master the Basics: Italian

  Includes index.
  1. Italian language — Grammar — 1950–   . I. Title.
PC1112.D35   1987   458.2′421   86-26607
ISBN 0-8120-3771-5

PRINTED IN THE UNITED STATES OF AMERICA

Contents

Special Topics   149

PREFACE

After having gone through the experience of studying a language for the first time, one invariably feels the need to do it all over again—to brush up one's grammar. Actually, this is a crucial stage in the process of learning another language. It gives you the opportunity to reflect upon what you know, to reinforce your skills, to fill in the gaps, to clarify difficult points—in sum, to help you build a more solid linguistic foundation.

This text is intended to give you the chance to brush up your Italian. It is written in a nontechnical, easy-to-read style. In fact, even the beginning learner would be able to work through the book without too much difficulty.

To find out how to use this book, just read ahead!

HOW TO USE THIS BOOK

This book can be used for both self-study and classroom learning. The first thing to do is to try the test provided for you in the "Find Out What You Know" part. This will give you not only the opportunity to "get into the action" right away, but it will also point out those areas where you are strong and those that need more study. At the end of the test there is a diagnostic summary that relates the questions to the chapters of this book.

The main part of this book is the "Grammar Brush-Up." This is divided into four sections: "The Basics," "Parts of Speech," "Special Topics," and "Verb Charts." If you are using this book for self-study, we suggest that you go through this part as though you were reading a story. The story in this case is the Italian language.

- In the "Basics" section you will find a nontechnical and easy-to-follow discussion of Italian sounds, spelling conventions, and word-order patterns. This section provides you with the main "story line" or "plot" of our language story.

- In the "Parts of Speech" section you will find the "main characters" of our story—the nouns, articles, pronouns, etc. that make up the Italian language.

- The "Special Topics" section contains the "supporting characters"—idiomatic expressions, numbers, synonyms, antonyms, etc.

- The "Verb Charts" section contains a list of common irregular verbs—the "evil characters."

Some chapters are longer than others and require both more time and more effort to learn. But never become discouraged! The explanations have been made as simple as possible. There are many charts and diagrams to help you "see" what is involved. And there are plenty of examples that illustrate each point. Only common vocabulary has been used throughout this book, and it is repeated frequently so that you will have a better opportunity to reinforce it. The topics in each chapter are numbered in order. This will allow you to go backward and forward in the book, and to relate grammatical points to each other. The numerical reference system for each section can be found at the start of the section.

The final part of this book is "Let's Review." You can do the 200 exercises and activities found in this section either after having read the "Grammatical Brush-Up" or as you work through the book. The questions are keyed to the numerical reference system in the "Answers" section. Another possibility is to do both: try the questions corresponding to each chapter after you have studied the chapter, and then do them again for a final review after you have finished working through the "brush-up." The 200 questions contain puzzles and humorous activities to help make the learning process as enjoyable as possible.

If you are using this book as a classroom text, the procedure just described is also applicable. However, your teacher undoubtedly will want to give you more chances to practice your Italian through other kinds of exercises and activities. Moreover, your teacher will certainly want to help you learn "the story of Italian" by elaborating upon and amplifying the book's explanations.

Now, let the story begin!

FIND OUT WHAT YOU KNOW

Let's get started with a test to help you pinpoint those areas in which you are strong and those in which you need some review. The following sixty questions correspond to the three main sections of this book:

- There are ten questions on the basics: the sounds, spelling conventions, and word-order patterns of Italian.
- There are forty questions on the parts of speech: the nouns, articles, pronouns, etc. of Italian.
- The last twenty questions will allow you to find out how much you remember about such special topics as telling time and counting in Italian.

At the end of the test, you will find the answers and an indication of where to go in this book to review and strengthen your weaker areas.

Test Yourself

THE BASICS

Each of the following four sentences contains one error. See if you can find the error, and then correct it.

1. Giovanni mangia tanta choccolata. _____
2. A jugno partiremo per l'Italia. _____
3. Mia madre è stanca e ha sono. _____
4. Andiamo al cinema ogni Mercoledì. _____

In the next two sentences there is one word that does not belong. Can you find the two extra words?

5. Maria aspetta per l'autobus. _____
6. Ogni sera mio padre ascolta a un programma italiano alla radio. _____

The next four sentences have something wrong with them. Rewrite each sentence correctly.

7. Il professore telefona suoi studenti.
   _____

8. Maria ha non scritto quella lettera.
   _____

9. Guida tua madre una FIAT?

_____

10. La ragazza è italiana che legge il giornale.

_____

PARTS OF SPEECH

Test your ability to form the plural of nouns. Which is the correct plural form for each of the following nouns?

11. ragazzo
    + ragazzi ☐
      ragazze ☐
      both ☐
12. artista
    + artisti ☐
      artiste ☐
      both ☐
13. automobile
      automobile ☐
    + automobili ☐
      both ☐
14. città
      città ☐
    + cittè ☐
      both ☐
15. uomo
    − uomi ☐
      uomini ☐
      both ☐

Match each definite article in the left column with an appropriate noun in the right column.

16. lo   figlio
    + l'   studentessa
      gli   amici
      il   amiche
      i   amico
      la   studente
      le   libri

Now match each indefinite article with the appropriate noun.

17. uno   automobile
    + una   specchio
      un'   occhio
      un   donna

Here's one more! Match each demonstrative with the appropriate noun.

18. quegli   entrata
    quell'   uscite
    questi   ragazzo
    quel   ragazzi
    questa   sbagli
    queste   penna

Now check the appropriate partitive plural for each of the
following nouns.

19. uno zio
    degli zii   ☐
    alcuni zii   ☐
    both   ☐
20. un'amica
    delle amiche   ☐
    qualche amica   ☐
    both   ☐

The adjectives in the following sentences do not have their
endings. Can you supply them?

21. Qual _____ libri hai comprato?
22. Quei ragazzi sono frances _____.
23. Anche quelle ragazze sono frances _____.
24. La lor _____ professoressa è italian _____.
25. Tutt _____ le studentesse in questa classe sono
    american _____.

The following pronouns are missing from sentences 26–31.
Can you put each one in its appropriate slot?

PRONOUNS: si, la, le, quella, il mio, chi

26. Il tuo orologio è bello, ma anche _____ è bello.
27. _____ ha mangiato tutti gli spaghetti?
28. Quale penna vuoi, questa o _____?
29. Hai chiamato Maria? Sì, _____ ho già chiamata.
30. Hai telefonato a Maria? Sì, _____ ho già telefonato.
31. Quei turisti _____ sono divertiti in Italia.

Can you match each subject pronoun with its verb?

32. io   avete dormito
    tu   mangiavano
    lei   capisco
    noi   dovrebbe studiare
    voi   siamo arrivati
    loro   scriverai

The following verbs are missing from the passage. Can you
put them in their appropriate slots?

> VERBS: avesse, sembrava, comprare, siamo andati,
> abbiamo comprato, conosceva

33. Ieri _____ ad un negozio a _____ delle
scarpe nuove. Il commesso ci _____. Era un vecchio amico di scuola. Benché _____ quarant'anni,
_____ ancora molto giovane. _____ due paia
di scarpe italiane.

Here are three adjectives. Check their corresponding
adverbs.

34. sincero
    sincermente ☐
    sinceramente ☐
35. facile
    facilmente ☐
    facilemente ☐
36. elegante
    elegantmente ☐
    elegantemente ☐

The following prepositions are missing from the passage.
Put them in their appropriate slots.

> PREPOSITIONS: fra, all', negli, del, di

37. Il figlio _____ signor Bianchi ha ventidue anni.
Studia _____ università _____ Bologna.
_____ due anni tornerà _____ Stati Uniti.

Check the appropriate answer to each question.

38. Giovanni, conosci qualcuno in questa città?
    No, non conosco nessuno. ☐
    No, non conosco niente. ☐
39. Dove sono i miei libri?
    Ci sono i tuoi libri. ☐
    Ecco i tuoi libri. ☐
40. Hai fatto lavare i piatti a tuo fratello?
    Sì, glieli ho fatti lavare. ☐
    Sì, li lava. ☐

SPECIAL TOPICS

Put *piace* and *piacciono* into the appropriate slots.

41. Non mi _____ quel programma televisivo. Mi _____
solo i film. Anche a te _____, non è vero?

There is an incorrect expression in each of the following two
groups. Which ones are they?

42. Maria ha fame. ☐
    Giovanni ha sete. ☐
    Il signore fa il biglietto. ☐
    Marco è freddo. ☐
43. Il professore è torto. ☐
    Il fumo mi dà fastidio. ☐
    Abbiamo bisogno di dormire. ☐
    Signora Binni, come sta? ☐

Fill in the missing parts.

44. 2.456 = due _____ quattro _____ cinquanta _____
45. Questa è la ventitr _____ volta che ti telefono!

Write out the following times.

46. 8:24 P.M. = _____.
47. 9:55 A.M. = _____.

Complete each sentence with the appropriate expression.

> EXPRESSIONS: il tre febbraio, maggio, autunno, fa
> freddo

48. Nel nord d'Italia il bel tempo non comincia prima
    di _____.
49. Le foglie degli alberi cadono ogni _____.
50. D'inverno _____.
51. Che data è oggi? _____.

Check the appropriate "conversation strategy."

52. It is the afternoon, and you meet someone. You might
    say:
    Buona notte ☐
    Buona sera ☐
    Buon giorno ☐
53. When answering the phone, you first say:
    Ciao. ☐
    Chi parla? ☐
    Pronto. ☐
54. To say "good-bye" to a friend, you might say:
    Ciao. ☐
    ArrivederLa. ☐
    Buon giorno. ☐

Can you match the synonyms in each column?

55. strada   sfortunatamente
    purtroppo   via
    uguale   lo stesso
    perciò   quindi

Now can you match the antonyms?

+ 56. alto   pieno
      fuori   basso
      vuoto   dentro
      ricco   povero

How good are you at translating? Try the following words. But be careful! There are some tricks in the sentences.

+ 57. (*This nation*) _____ è molto bella.
+ 58. (*My parents*) _____ abitano in Italia.
+ 59. Devo andare (*to the library*) _____ per studiare un po'.
- 60. Ho già letto (*that magazine*) _____.

Answers

1. cioccolata
2. giugno
3. sonno
4. mercoledì
   (not capitalized)
5. per
6. a
7. Il professore telefona *ai* suoi studenti.
8. Maria non ha scritto quella lettera.
9. Tua madre guida una FIAT?/Guida una FIAT, tua madre?
10. La ragazza che legge il giornale è italiana.
11. ragazzi
12. both
13. automobili
14. città
15. uomini
16. lo studente
    l'amico
    gli amici
    il figlio
    i libri
    la studentessa
    le amiche
17. uno specchio
    una donna
    un'automobile
    un occhio
18. quegli sbagli
    quell'entrata
    questi ragazzi
    quel ragazzo
    questa penna
    queste uscite
19. both
20. both
21. Quali
22. francesi
23. francesi
24. loro/italiana
25. Tutte/americane
26. il mio
27. Chi
28. quella
29. la
30. le
31. si
32. io capisco
    tu scriverai
    lei dovrebbe studiare
    noi siamo arrivati
    voi avete dormito
    loro mangiavano
33. siamo andati; comprare; conosceva; avesse; sembrava; Abbiamo comprato

34. sinceramente
35. facilmente
36. elegantemente
37. *del* signor Bianchi;
    *all'*università *di* Bologna;
    Fra due anni; *negli*
    Stati Uniti.
38. No, non conosco
    nessuno.
39. Ecco i tuoi libri.
40. Sì, glieli ho fatti lavare.
41. Non mi *piace* quel
    programma televisivo.
    Mi *piacciono* solo i film.
    Anche a te *piacciono,*
    non è vero?
42. "Marco è freddo."
43. "Il professore è torto."
44. due*mila* quattro*cento*
    cinquanta*sei*
45. ventitre*esima*
46. le otto e ventiquattro di
    sera / le venti e
    ventiquattro
47. le dieci meno cinque /
    le nove e cinquantacinque
48. maggio
49. autunno
50. fa freddo
51. Il tre febbraio.
52. Buona sera.
53. Pronto.
54. Ciao.
55. strada — via
    purtroppo —
    sfortunatamente
    uguale — lo stesso
    perciò — quindi
56. alto — basso
    fuori — dentro
    vuoto — pieno
    ricco — povero
57. Questa nazione
58. I miei genitori
59. alla biblioteca
60. quella rivista

Diagnostic Analysis

Section	Question numbers	Number of Answers	
		Right	Wrong
THE BASICS			
1. Italian Sounds and Spelling	1, 2, 3, 4	1	3
2. Elements of an Italian Sentence	5, 6, 7, 8, 9, 10	5	1
THE PARTS OF SPEECH			
3. Nouns	11, 12, 13, 14, 15	4	1
4. Articles	16, 17, 18	3	0
5. Partitives	19, 20	0	2

Section	Question numbers	Number of Answers	
		Right	Wrong
THE BASICS			
6. Adjectives	21, 22, 23, 24, 25	3	2
7. Pronouns	26, 27, 28, 29, 30, 31	6	0
8. Verbs	32, 33	2	0
9. Adverbs	34, 35, 36	2	1
10. Prepositions	37	1	0
11. Negatives and Other Grammatical Points	38, 39, 40	3	0
SPECIAL TOPICS			
12. The Verb "Piacere"	41	0	1
13. Idioms	42, 43	0	2
14. Numbers	44, 45	1	1
15. Telling Time	46, 47	0	2
16. Days, Months, Seasons, Dates, Weather	48, 49, 50, 51	4	0
17. Common Conversation Techniques	52, 53, 54	3	0
18. Synonyms and Antonyms	55, 56	1	1
19. Cognates	57, 58, 59, 60	3	1
TOTAL QUESTIONS:	60	42	18

Use the following scale to see how you did.

58 to 60 right:	**Excellent**
55 to 57 right:	**Very Good**
52 to 54 right:	**Average**
49 to 51 right:	**Below Average**
Fewer than 49 right:	**Unsatisfactory**

A GRAMMAR BRUSH-UP
The Basics

§1.

Guide to Italian Sounds and Spelling

§1.1
WHAT ARE VOWELS AND CONSONANTS?

There are two kinds of sounds in any language.

- *Vowels* are produced by air passing out through the mouth without being blocked. The letters that represent these sounds are: *a, e, i, o, u.*

- *Consonants,* on the other hand, are produced by blockage (partial or complete) of the air. The remaining alphabet letters are used to represent consonant sounds: *b, c, d,* etc.

§1.2
VOWELS

Italian vowels should not cause you any problems.

Alphabet Letters	Sounds	Examples
a	Similar to the *a* sound in "father," or to the exclamation "ah!"	*casa*/ house *acqua*/ water
e	Similar to the *e* sound in "bet," or to the exclamation "eh!"	*bene*/well *esame*/ exam
i	Similar to the *i* sound in machine	*vini*/wines *indirizzi*/ addresses
o	Similar to the *o* sound in "sorry," or to the exclamation "oh!"	*otto*/eight *oro*/gold
u	Similar to the *oo* sound in "*boot*," or to the exclamation "ooh!"	*uva*/ grapes *gusto*/ taste

- Speakers in various parts of Italy pronounce *e* and *o* differently. In some parts, these vowels are pronounced with the mouth relatively more open. In others, they are pronounced with the mouth relatively more closed. In many areas, however, *both* pronunciations are used.

- To get an idea of what this means, consider how the *a* in "tomato" is pronounced in North America. In some areas, it is pronounced like the *a* in "father." In other areas, it is pronounced like the *a* in "pay." However, whether it is pronounced one way or the other, no one will have much difficulty understanding that the word is "tomato." This is exactly what happens in the case of Italian *e* and *o*.

- The letter *i* stands for the semivowel sounds similar to those represented by the *y* in "yes" and "say."

Words Pronounced Like "yes"	Words Pronounced Like "say"
ieri/yesterday	*mai*/ever, never
piatto/plate	*poi*/then

- This pronunciation feature occurs when the *i* is next to another vowel and both are pronounced rapidly together. If there is a slight pause between the two vowels, then pronounce *i* in its normal way as in the word *zio* (uncle).

- Similarly, the letter *u* stands for the semivowel sounds represented by the *w* in "way" and "how."

Words Pronounced Like "way"	Words Pronounced Like "how"
uomo/man	*causa*/cause
buono/good	*laurea*/degree (university)

- Once again, this feature occurs when the *u* is next to another vowel and both are pronounced rapidly together.

§1.3 CONSONANTS

The following Italian consonants should cause you few problems

Alphabet Letters	Sounds	Examples
b	Identical to the *b* sound in "*boy*."	*bello*/beautiful *bravo*/good
d	Identical to the *d* sound in "*day*." This is true even when followed by *r*; in English, the tongue is raised a bit more: "*drop*."	*dopo*/after la*dro*/thief

Alphabet Letters	Sounds	Examples
f	Identical to the *f* sound in *"fun."*	*forte*/strong *frutta*/fruit
l	Identical to the *l* sound in *"love."* This is true even when it comes at the end of a word or syllable; in English, the back of the tongue is raised a bit more: "bi*l*."	*latte*/milk a*l*to/tall
m	Identical to the *m* sound in *"more."*	*matita*/pencil *mondo*/world
n	Identical to the *n* sound in *"nose."*	*naso*/nose *nono*/ninth
p	Identical to the *p* sound in *"price."*	*porta*/door *prezzo*/price
q	Identical to the *q* sound in *"quick."* It is always followed by *u*.	*quanto*/how much *quinto*/fifth
r	Like a "rolled" *r* sound (as in some Scottish dialects). Pronounced with flip of tongue against the upper gums.	*rosso*/red *raro*/rare
t	Like the *t* sound in *"fat"* (with the tongue against the upper teeth).	*tardi*/late *tu*/you
v	Identical to the *v* sound in *"vine."*	*vino*/wine

The following consonants are pronounced in different ways, as explained in the chart:

Alphabet Letters	Sounds	Examples
c	Represents the *k* sound in *"kit"* and *"cat."* Used in front of *a, o, u,* and any consonant.	Before *a, o, u:* *cane*/dog *come*/how *cuore*/heart Before any consonant: *classe*/class *cravatta*/tie

Alphabet Letters	Sounds	Examples
ch	Represents the same *k* sound. Used in front of *e* and *i*.	*che*/what *chi*/who *chi*esa/church
c	Represents the *ch* sound in "*ch*urch" when used in front of *e* and *i*.	*c*ena/dinner *c*inema/movies
ci	Represents the *ch* sound (as in "so*ci*al") when used in front of *a, o, u*.	*ci*ao/hi, bye *ci*occolata/chocolate
g	Represents the *g* sound in "*g*ood." Used in front of *a, o, u,* and any consonant.	Before a, o, u: *g*atto/cat *g*ola/throat *gu*anto/glove Before any consonant: *g*loria/glory *g*rande/big, large
gh	Represents the same *g* sound. Used in front of *e* and *o*.	spa*gh*etti/spaghetti *gh*iaccio/ice
g	Represents the *j* sound in "*j*ust." Used in front of *e* and *i*.	*g*ente/people *g*iro/turn, tour
gi	Represents the same *j* sound. Used in front of *a, o, u*.	*gi*acca/jacket *gi*orno/day *giu*gno/June
sc	Represents the sound sequence *sk* in front of *a, o, u,* or any consonant.	*sc*ala/staircase *sc*opa/broom *scu*ola/school *sc*rivere/to write
sch	Represents the same *sk* sequence in front of *e* and *i*.	*sch*erzo/prank *sch*ifo/disgust
sc	Represents the *sh* sound in front of *e* and *i*.	*sc*ena/scene
sci	Represents the same *sh* sound in front of *a, o, u*.	*sci*opero/labor strike *sciu*pare/to waste

- The sound represented by *gli* is similar to the *lli* in "million":

  fi*gli*o / son
  lu*gli*o / July

- The sound represented by *gn* is similar to the *ny* of "canyon":

  so*gn*o / dream
  giu*gn*o / June

- The letter *s* can stand for both the *s* sound in "sip" or the *z* sound in "zip." The *z* sound occurs before *b, d, g, l, m, n, r, v;* otherwise, the *s* sound is used.

  EXAMPLES

s-sound	z-sound
sapone / soap	*sbaglio* / mistake
stanco / tired	*smettere* / to stop
sete / thirst	*svegliarsi* / to wake up
specchio / mirror	*slittare* / to slide

- When *s* occurs between vowels, either sound may be used.

  casa / house

  s   z

- The letter *z* stands for the *ts* sound in "ca*ts*" or the *ds* sound in "la*ds*":

  zio / uncle

  ts   ds

- The letter *h* does not represent any sound. It is like the silent *h* of "*h*our": *ho* (I have) (pronounced "oh!").

- Any one of these consonants can have a corresponding double consonant. The pronunciation of double consonants simply lasts twice as long as the corresponding single consonant.

  EXAMPLES

Single Consonant	Corresponding Double
fato / fate	*fatto* / fact
caro / dear	*carro* / cart
pala / shovel	*palla* / ball
sono / I am	*sonno* / sleep

§1.4 STRESS

Knowing where to put the stress, or main accent, on an Italian word is not always easy, but you can always look up a word you are unsure of in a dictionary that indicates stress.
Here are some general guidelines:

- In many words, the stress falls on the next-to-last syllable. You can identify most syllables easily because they contain a vowel.

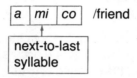

- But be careful! This is not always the case.

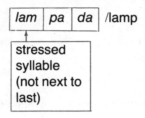

- Some words show an accent mark on the final vowel. This is, of course, where you put the stress.

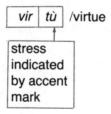

- The accent mark in Italian can always be made to slant to the left (à). However, in words ending in -ché, it normally slants to the right:

EXAMPLES

perché (OR *perchè*)	why, because
benché (OR *benchè*)	although

§1.5 SPELLING CONVENTIONS

To spell Italian words, just follow the guidelines described in the previous sections. Italian also uses the same punctuation marks as English.
The Italian alphabet does not have the letters *j, k, w, x,* and *y*. These are found, however, in words that Italian has borrowed from other languages, primarily English.

EXAMPLES

il karatè	karate
il jazz	jazz
il weekend	weekend
lo yacht	yacht

Like English, capital letters are used at the beginning of sentences and with proper nouns (see §3.1). However, there are a few conventions worth noting.

- The pronoun *io*/I is not capitalized (unless it is the first word of a sentence).

  Vengo anche io.   I'm coming too.

- Titles are not usually capitalized.

  il professor Verdi   Professor Verdi
  la dottoressa Martini   Dr. Martini

- Adjectives and nouns referring to languages and nationality are not capitalized.

  È un italiano. / He is an Italian.
  La lingua spagnola è interessante. / The Spanish language is interesting.

- Names of the seasons, months of the year, and days of the week also are not capitalized.

  la primavera   spring
  mercoledì   Tuesday
  maggio   May

§2.

Summaries of Word Order in an Italian Sentence

§2.1
WHAT IS A
SENTENCE?

A *sentence* is an organized series of words that allows us to make a statement, ask a question, express a thought, offer an opinion, etc. In writing, a sentence is easily identified because it starts with a capitalized word and ends with either a period, a question mark, or an exclamation mark.

EXAMPLES

Quella donna è italiana. / That woman is Italian. (statement)
È italiana, quella donna? / Is that woman Italian? (question)
Penso che quella donna sia italiana. / I think that woman is Italian. (thought/opinion)

- Notice that the way in which a sentence is organized is related to what you intend to say and how you are going to say it. You cannot put words in just any order!

  donna è italiana quella   Quella donna è italiana.

Sentences have two basic parts: a *subject* and a *predicate*.

- A *subject* is "who" or "what" the sentence is about. It is often the first element in a simple sentence.

EXAMPLES

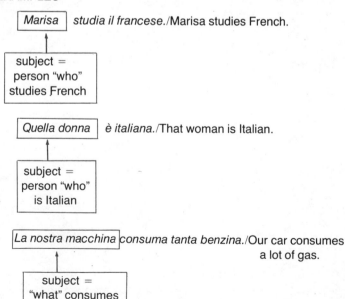

| Marisa | studia il francese./Marisa studies French. |

subject =
person "who"
studies French

| Quella donna | è italiana./That woman is Italian. |

subject =
person "who"
is Italian

| La nostra macchina | consuma tanta benzina./Our car consumes a lot of gas. |

subject =
"what" consumes
too much gas

16

● But be careful! The subject is not always the first element.

EXAMPLES

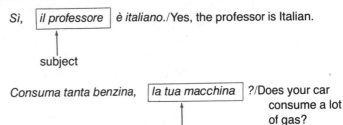

Sì, | *il professore* | *è italiano.*/Yes, the professor is Italian.

subject

Consuma tanta benzina, | *la tua macchina* | ?/Does your car consume a lot of gas?

subject

● A *predicate* is the remaining part of the sentence that expresses what is said about the subject. In many simple sentences, you will find it after the subject.

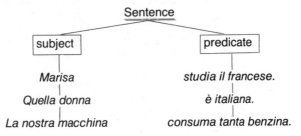

Sentence

subject   predicate

Marisa   *studia il francese.*

Quella donna   *è italiana.*

La nostra macchina   *consuma tanta benzina.*

● A main subject will, of course, have a main predicate.

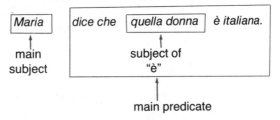

Maria | *dice che* | *quella donna* | *è italiana.*

main subject   subject of "è"

main predicate

● A subject must contain a noun (see Chapter 3) or pronoun (see Chapter 7); a predicate must include a verb (see Chapter 8). The parts of speech that make up the subject and predicate are defined and discussed in Chapters 3 to 11.

§2.2
SENTENCES
BY FUNCTION

§2.2 – 1
Affirmative

This type of sentence states or affirms something in a positive way.

EXAMPLES

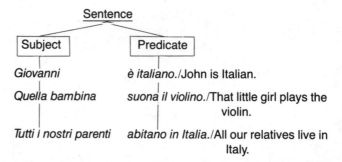

Sentence

Subject	Predicate
Giovanni	*è italiano.*/John is Italian.
Quella bambina	*suona il violino.*/That little girl plays the violin.
Tutti i nostri parenti	*abitano in Italia.*/All our relatives live in Italy.

- The predicate of such sentences may or may not have an object. An *object* is the noun or noun phrase that receives the action, and normally follows a verb. A *noun phrase* consists of a noun accompanied by an article and, possibly, an adjective. An object can also be a pronoun that replaces the noun or noun phrase.

- There are two types of objects: *direct* and *indirect*. These can be identified very easily as follows:

> A noun, or noun phrase, that directly follows the verb is a *direct object*.

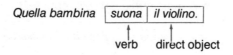

Quella bambina | suona | il violino.
              verb direct object

> A noun, or noun phrase, that follows the verb but is introduced by the preposition *a* (to, at) is an *indirect object*.

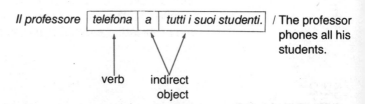

Il professore | telefona | a | tutti i suoi studenti. | / The professor phones all his students.
         verb   indirect object

- Whether an object is direct or indirect depends on the verb. Some verbs must be followed only by one type of object or the other. Fortunately, most verbs in Italian match their English equivalents when it comes to whether or not a direct or indirect object should follow.

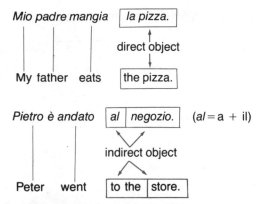

- However, there are some special cases! Here are the most important ones.

Verbs Requiring a Direct Object
ascoltare/to listen (to)   *Mia madre ascolta la radio ogni sera.*/My mother listens to the radio every evening.
aspettare/to wait (for)   *Maria aspetta l'autobus.*/Mary is waiting for the bus.
cercare/to search, look (for)   *Tina cerca la sua borsa.*/Tina is looking for her purse.

- One way to remember these differences is to view the Italian verb as "containing" the preposition.

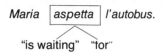

Verbs Requiring an Indirect Object
chiedere/domandare (a)/to ask (someone)   *Gino chiede al professore di venire alla festa.*/   Gino asks the professor to come to the party.
telefonare (a)/to phone   *Gina telefona a sua madre.*/Gina phones her mother.
rispondere (a)/to answer   *La studentessa risponde alla domanda.*/The student answers the question.

- Some verbs can take both kinds of objects.

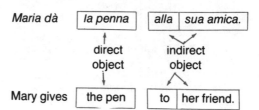

- As mentioned earlier, it is not always necessary to have an object in a sentence.

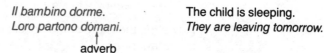

Il bambino dorme.	The child is sleeping.
Loro partono domani.	*They are leaving tomorrow.*

---

§2.2 – 2 Negative

To make any sentence negative in Italian, just put *non* before the predicate.

EXAMPLES

Affirmative	Negative
Maria aspetta l'autobus. / Mary is waiting for the bus.	*Maria non aspetta l'autobus.* / Mary is not waiting for the bus.
Il bambino dorme. / The child is sleeping.	*Il bambino non dorme.* / The child is not sleeping.
Maria mi dà la mela. / Mary gives me the apple.	*Maria non mi dà la mela.* / Mary does not give me the apple.

- Notice that the pronoun *mi*, which is still part of the predicate, comes before the verb, (see §7.3.1).

- And do not forget to say "yes" and "no."

sì/yes *Sì, Gina aspetta il suo amico.*/Yes, Gina is waiting for her friend.
no/no *No, Gina non aspetta il suo amico.*/No, Gina is not waiting for her friend.

- Other negatives are discussed in Chapter 11.

---

§2.2 – 3 Interrogative

An interrogative sentence allows you to ask a question. In writing, it always has a question mark at the end. In Italian the two most common methods of turning an affirmative sentence into an interrogative one are:

> Simply put a question mark at the end. In speaking, the voice goes up at the end of the sentence as in English.

EXAMPLES

Affirmative	Interrogative
Anna cerca il gatto. /	*Anna cerca il gatto?* /
Ann is looking for the cat.	Ann is looking for the cat?
Il bambino dorme. /	*Il bambino dorme?* /
The child is sleeping.	The child is sleeping?

> Put the subject at the end of the sentence, adding a question mark.

EXAMPLES

subject

Marco *ascolta la musica.*/Mark is listening to the music.

Ascolta la musica Marco *?*/Is Mark listening to the music?

subject

Il bambino *dorme.*/The child is sleeping.

Dorme il bambino *?*/Is the child sleeping?

Interrogative sentences can also be formed by using interrogative adjectives (see §6.4 – 2) or pronouns (see §7.2). These allow you to ask "what?," "when?," "where?," etc.

EXAMPLES

| *Quale macchina preferisci?* / | Which car do you prefer? |
| *Come va?* / | How's it going? |

More will be said about these in the appropriate chapters. Use either *no?*, *vero?*, or *non è vero?* to express the following:

Giovanni è italiano, { *no?* / *vero?* / *non è vero?* }

John is Italian, isn't he?

Tua madre guida una macchina sportiva, { *no?* / *vero?* / *non è vero?* }

Your mother drives a sports car, doesn't she?

§2.2 – 4
Emphatic

To put emphasis on the subject of a sentence, all you have to do is put the subject at the end. In writing you must, of course, add an exclamation mark.

> | *Luisa* | *ha pagato il conto*/Louise paid the bill.

> *Ha pagato il conto,* | *Luisa* | *!*/Louise paid the bill!

> | *Il dottore* | *l'ha detto.*/The doctor said it.

> *L'ha detto* | *il dottore* | *!*/The doctor said it!

The imperative forms of the verb also are used for adding emphasis (see §8.3).

> *Anna, paga il conto!* / Ann, pay the bill!

§2.3
SENTENCES BY STRUCTURE

§2.3 – 1
Simple

A simple sentence has only *one* (main) subject and *one* (main) predicate.

§2.3 – 2
Complex

A complex sentence has one main clause and at least one subordinate, or dependent, clause. It still has a main subject and predicate.

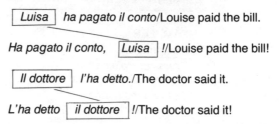

> | *La ragazza* | *che legge il giornale* | *è francese.* | /The girl who is reading the newspaper is French.
>
> main subject   main predicate

(a) Relative Clauses

A *clause* is a group of related words that contains a subject and predicate and is part of the main sentence. A *relative clause* is a dependent clause introduced by a relative pronoun. (see §7.4).

Main sentence: *La ragazza è italiana.*/The girl is Italian.
Sentence to be changed into a clause:

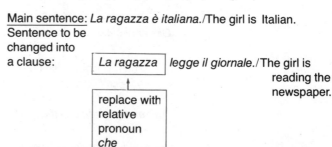

> | *La ragazza* | *legge il giornale.*/The girl is reading the newspaper.
>
> replace with relative pronoun *che*

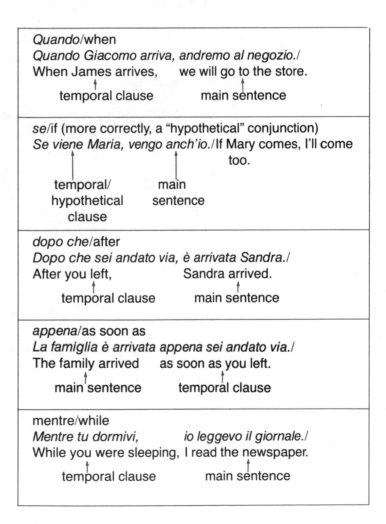

Result:
(complex
sentence)

| *La ragazza* | *che* | *legge il giornale* | *è italiana.* |

main
subject

relative
pronoun

relative
clause

main
predicate

(b) Temporal Clauses

Temporal clauses are introduced by subordinating conjunctions. A *conjunction* is a word that connects words, phrases, and clauses. Temporal means that it expresses a time relationship. The main subordinating conjunctions are:

Quando/when
Quando Giacomo arriva, andremo al negozio./
When James arrives,   we will go to the store.

    temporal clause   main sentence

---

se/if (more correctly, a "hypothetical" conjunction)
Se viene Maria, vengo anch'io./If Mary comes, I'll come too.

    temporal/   main
    hypothetical   sentence
    clause

---

dopo che/after
Dopo che sei andato via, è arrivata Sandra./
After you left,   Sandra arrived.

    temporal clause   main sentence

---

appena/as soon as
La famiglia è arrivata appena sei andato via./
The family arrived   as soon as you left.

    main sentence   temporal clause

---

mentre/while
Mentre tu dormivi,   io leggevo il giornale./
While you were sleeping, I read the newspaper.

    temporal clause   main sentence

Notice that these have exact equivalents in English.

(c) Other Types of Conjunctions
Other kinds of conjunctions can also introduce clauses into sentences.

Benché piova, esco lo stesso./Although it is raining, I'm going
out just the same.

↑
conjunction

A number of these require the *subjunctive* form of the verb, and thus will be discussed in the sections dealing with the subjunctive (see §8.5).

To join two sentences, two clauses, two words, etc., simply use the conjunctions *e*/and or *o*/or.

EXAMPLES

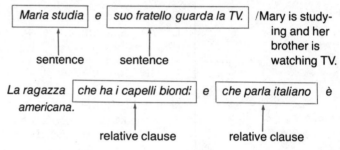

| Maria studia | e | suo fratello guarda la TV. | /Mary is study-
ing and her
brother is
watching TV.

↑   ↑
sentence   sentence

La ragazza | che ha i capelli biondi | e | che parla italiano | è
americana.

↑   ↑
relative clause   relative clause

The girl who has blonde hair and who speaks Italian is American.

| Gino | e | Gina | parlano italiano./Gino and Gina speak
Italian.

↑   ↑
noun   noun

Vengo | con la macchina | o | a piedi | ./I'm coming with the
car or on foot.

↑   ↑
phrase   phrase

§2.4 INCOMPLETE SENTENCES

When we speak, we don't always use complete sentences, that is, a sentence with a subject and predicate. Either part of a sentence may be left out when it is clearly implied.

Complete Sentence   Incomplete Sentence

| *Come stai?*/How are you? |

Sto bene, grazie. / I am well, thanks.←→*Bene, grazie.* / Well, thanks.

> *Chi è arrivato in ritardo?*/Who arrived late?

Mio padre è arrivato in ritardo./ ←————→ *Mio padre.*/My father.
My father arrived late.

> Quando sei andato al teatro?/When did you go to the
> theater?

Ieri sono andato al teatro./←————→ *Ieri.*/Yesterday.
Yesterday I went to the
theater.

§2.5
Active versus
Passive
Sentences

All the sentences used so far are *active* sentences — the verb always expresses the action performed by the subject. But for many active sentences there are corresponding *passive* ones in which the action is performed *on* the subject. (The passive voice, however, is found less frequently in the Italian than in English.)

Active	Passive
Maria legge il libro. / Mary reads the book.	*Il libro è letto da Maria.* / The book is read by Mary.

You will learn how to change active sentences into passive ones in Section §8.8.

§2.6
Direct and
Indirect
Sentences

Sentences can be subdivided into two general categories: direct speech and indirect speech. *Direct* speech occurs when talking directly to someone. *Indirect* speech occurs when talking about someone or something. Notice that there are differences between the two forms of speech (e.g. the "article" is dropped in direct speech).

Indirect	Direct
Carlo dice che i ragazzi sono italiani.	*Carlo chiede, "Ragazzi, siete italiani?"*
Carlo says that the boys are Italian.	Carlo asks, "Boys, are you Italian?"

Parts of Speech

§3.

NOUNS

§3.1
**WHAT ARE
NOUNS?**

Nouns are words that allow us to name and label the persons, objects, places, concepts, etc., that make up our world. In Italian, a noun generally can be recognized by its vowel ending, which indicates the gender (see §3.2) and number (see §3.3) of the noun.

EXAMPLES

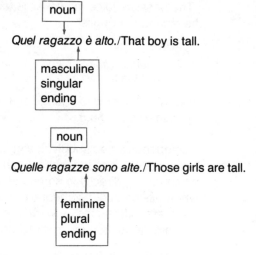

There are two main types of nouns:

● *Proper* nouns are the names given to people and places. They are always capitalized.

EXAMPLES

Il signor Rossi è simpatico./Mr. Rossi is pleasant.

Maria è felice./Mary is happy.

L'Italia è bella./Italy is beautiful.

- *Common* nouns are all the other kinds of nouns used in a language. These can be "count" or "noncount."

- Count nouns refer to persons, things, etc., that can be counted. They have both a singular and plural form.

  EXAMPLES

Singular	Plural
il libro / the book	*i libri* / the books
la penna / the pen	*le penne* / the pens

- Noncount nouns refer to persons, things, etc., that cannot be counted, and therefore normally have only a singular form.

  EXAMPLES

  l'acqua / water
  lo zucchero / sugar
  il pane / bread

- Some noncount nouns can, of course, be used in a figurative way in the same manner as count nouns.

  EXAMPLE

  le acque del mare / the waters of the sea

- Common nouns are not capitalized unless they occur at the beginning of a sentence. Nouns referring to languages, speakers of a language, or inhabitants of an area normally are not capitalized.

  EXAMPLES

  L'italiano è una bella lingua. / Italian is a beautiful language.
  Ci sono tanti spagnoli in quella città. / There are lots of Spaniards in that city.

  However, there is a tendency now to imitate the English practice of capitalizing such nouns.
  To summarize:

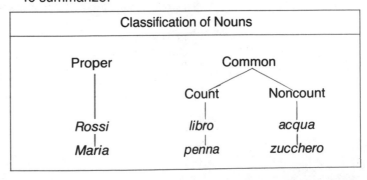

§3.2 GENDER

Italian nouns have two genders: masculine and feminine. More will be said about genders in the next section (see §3.2–1). For now, it is important to know that this system of classification determines the form of both the articles (see Chapter 4) and adjectives (see Chapter 6) that accompany nouns in speech.

The ending of a noun gives us an important clue as to its gender.

- Nouns ending with the vowel -*o* are normally masculine.

EXAMPLES

il ragazzo / the boy
il giorno / the day
l'aeroporto / the airport
Carlo / Charles
Belgio / Belgium

- Nouns ending with the vowel -*a* are normally feminine.

EXAMPLES

la ragazza / the girl
la carta / the paper
la valigia / the suitcase
Carla / Carla
l'Italia / Italy

- Nouns ending with the vowel -*e* are either masculine or feminine. To be sure about the gender of a specific noun ending in -*e*, you will have to consult a dictionary.

EXAMPLES

Masculine	Feminine
dottore / doctor	*gente* / people
padre / father	*madre* / mother
nome / name	*televisione* / television
Giuseppe / Joseph	*notte* / night

- In normal speech, the gender of a common noun often can be determined by the form of its modifiers.

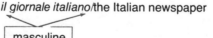
il giornale italiano/the Italian newspaper

```
masculine
singular
forms
```

la notte lunga/the long night

```
feminine
singular
forms
```

Nouns that have the above characteristics are referred to as regular nouns.

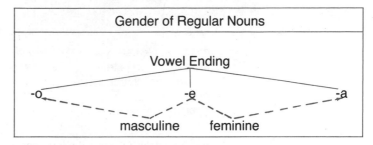

§3.2 – 1
Some Gender
Patterns

The assigning of genders to nouns, especially those referring to an object or concept, is arbitrary, so it is not always possible, on the basis of the noun's meaning, to determine whether it will have a masculine or feminine ending. Noun endings, however, do reflect biological gender (i.e., sex). In general, male beings are designated by nouns ending in -o or -e (masculine endings); and female beings are designated by nouns ending in -a or -e (feminine endings).

EXAMPLES

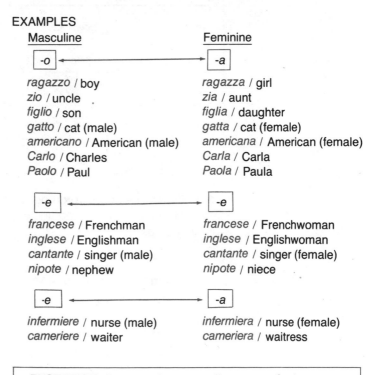

Masculine	Feminine
-o	**-a**
ragazzo / boy	*ragazza* / girl
zio / uncle	*zia* / aunt
figlio / son	*figlia* / daughter
gatto / cat (male)	*gatta* / cat (female)
americano / American (male)	*americana* / American (female)
Carlo / Charles	*Carla* / Carla
Paolo / Paul	*Paola* / Paula
-e	**-e**
francese / Frenchman	*francese* / Frenchwoman
inglese / Englishman	*inglese* / Englishwoman
cantante / singer (male)	*cantante* / singer (female)
nipote / nephew	*nipote* / niece
-e	**-a**
infermiere / nurse (male)	*infermiera* / nurse (female)
cameriere / waiter	*cameriera* / waitress

EXCEPTION: *Il soprano* is a masculine noun referring to a female person.

Following are some other interesting patterns.

- In general, the names of trees are masculine, whereas the fruit they bear is feminine.

EXAMPLES

Masculine	Feminine
melo / apple tree	*mela* / apple
arancio / orange tree	*arancia* / orange
pesco / peach tree	*pesca* / peach
pero / pear tree	*pera* / pear
ciliegio / cherry tree	*ciliegia* / cherry

> EXCEPTIONS: *Limone* (lemon), *fico* (fig), and *mandarino* (mandarin) refer to both the tree and the fruit.

- Masculine nouns ending in *-tore* referring to male persons often have corresponding feminine nouns ending in *-trice* referring to female persons.

Masculine	Feminine	Translation
genitore	genitrice	parent
pittore	pittrice	painter
autore	autrice	author
attore	attrice	actor/actress
scultore	scultrice	sculptor/sculptress

- Some masculine nouns referring to male beings have corresponding feminine nouns ending in *-essa* referring to female beings.

Masculine	Feminine	Translation
dottore	dottoressa	doctor
professore	professoressa	professor
avvocato	avvocatessa	lawyer
elefante	elefantessa	elephant

§3.2 – 2
Nouns Ending in -*ista*

These nouns generally refer to professional persons. They can be either masculine (even if they end in -*a*) or feminine, according to whether they designate a male or female person.

Masculine	Feminine	Translation
il dentista	la dentista	dentist
il pianista	la pianista	pianist
il farmacista	la farmacista	pharmacist
il violinista	la violinista	violinist

§3.2 – 3
Nouns Ending in an Accented Vowel

A few Italian nouns end in an accented vowel. In general, those nouns ending in -*à* and -*ù* are feminine; the others are masculine.

EXAMPLES

Masculine
il tè / the tea
il caffè / the coffee
il lunedì / Monday
il tassì / the taxi

Feminine
la città / the city
l'università / the university
la gioventù / the youth
la virtù / virtue

> EXCEPTIONS: There are several exceptions to this pattern, notably *il papà* (father/dad) (= masculine).

§3.2 – 4
Borrowed Nouns

These are nouns that have been borrowed from other languages, primarily English. Unless they refer to a female being (e.g., *hostess*), they are all treated as masculine nouns.

EXAMPLES
lo sport / sport
il tram / streetcar
il computer / computer
il clacson / car horn
il tennis / tennis
l'autobus / bus

§3.2 – 5
Nouns Ending in -*ema* and -*amma*

These nouns correspond to English nouns ending in -*em* and -*am*, and are of Greek origin. They all are masculine, even if they end in -*a*.

EXAMPLES
il problema / the problem
il teorema / the theorem
il programma / the program
il telegramma / the telegram
il diagramma / the diagram

§3.2 – 6 Nouns Ending in -si

These nouns correspond to English nouns ending in *-sis*, and also are of Greek origin. They all are feminine.

la crisi / the crisis
la tesi / the thesis
l'analisi / the analysis
l'ipotesi / the hypothesis

> EXCEPTION: *Il brindisi* ([drinking] toast) is masculine and is of Germanic origin.

§3.3 NUMBER

Number means that a word can be *singular* (= referring to one person, thing, etc.) or *plural* (= referring to more than one). Recall that noncount nouns (see §3.1) have only a singular form.

EXAMPLES
l'acqua / water
il pane / bread
la fame / hunger
la sete / thirst
il pepe / pepper
il sale / salt

A few nouns occur only in the plural form. They refer to things made up of more than one part.

EXAMPLES
le forbici / scissors
gli occhiali / (eye)glasses
i pantaloni / pants
le mutande / underwear
i baffi / moustache

§3.3 – 1 Plural of Regular Nouns

Common count nouns have both a singular and plural form. Regular Italian nouns (see §3.2) are put into the plural by making the following changes to the vowel endings.

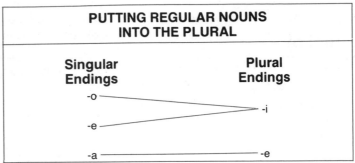

PUTTING REGULAR NOUNS
INTO THE PLURAL

Singular Endings	**Plural Endings**
-o	-i
-e	
-a	-e

EXAMPLES

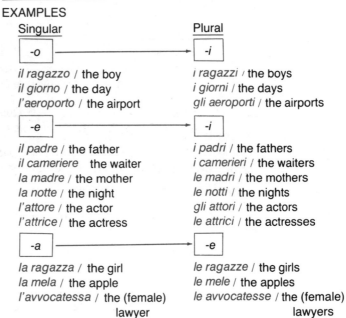

Singular | Plural

-o ⟶ -i

il ragazzo / the boy | *i ragazzi* / the boys
il giorno / the day | *i giorni* / the days
l'aeroporto / the airport | *gli aeroporti* / the airports

-e ⟶ -i

il padre / the father | *i padri* / the fathers
il cameriere the waiter | *i camerieri* / the waiters
la madre / the mother | *le madri* / the mothers
la notte / the night | *le notti* / the nights
l'attore / the actor | *gli attori* / the actors
l'attrice / the actress | *le attrici* / the actresses

-a ⟶ -e

la ragazza / the girl | *le ragazze* / the girls
la mela / the apple | *le mele* / the apples
l'avvocatessa / the (female) lawyer | *le avvocatesse* / the (female) lawyers

- Be careful! The noun *gente* (people) is singular in Italian.

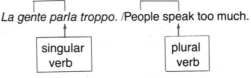

La gente parla troppo. /People speak too much.

| singular verb | plural verb |

- Note that the plural ending *-i* is used when the noun refers to both male *and* female beings.

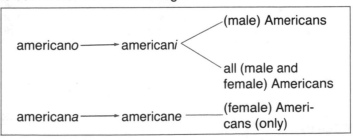

americano ⟶ americani ⟨ (male) Americans / all (male and female) Americans

americana ⟶ americane ⟶ (female) Americans (only)

§3.3 – 2 Plural of Nouns Ending in -*ista*, -*ema*, and -*amma*

Nouns ending in -*ista* are either masculine or feminine (see §3.2–2). The plural of such nouns is obtained as follows:

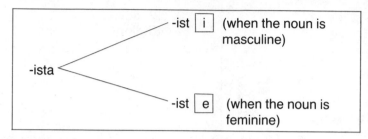

EXAMPLES

Singular		Plural	
il dentista	the (male) dentist	*i dentisti*	the (male) dentists
la dentista	the (female) dentist	*le dentiste*	the (female) dentists
il turista	the (male) tourist	*i turisti*	the (male) tourists
la turista	the (female) tourist	*le turiste*	the (male) tourists

- Note that in this case as well, the plural ending -*i* is used to designate both male and female beings.

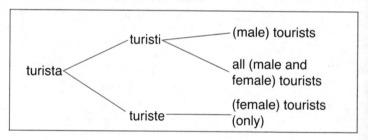

All nouns ending in -*ema* and -*amma* are masculine (see §3.2–5). The plural of such nouns is obtained as follows.

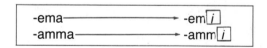

EXAMPLES

Singular		Plural	
il problema	/ the problem	*i problemi*	/ the problems
il programma	/ the program	*i programmi*	/ the programs
il diagramma	/ the diagram	*i diagrammi*	/ the diagrams

§3.3 – 3 Plural of Other Nouns

Nouns ending in -*si* (see §3.2–6) and in an accented vowel (see §3.2–3), as well as borrowed nouns (see §3.2–4) (and all nouns ending in a consonant), do *not* undergo any changes in the plural.

EXAMPLES

Singular	Plural
la città / the city	*le città* / the cities
il computer / the computer	*i computer* / the computers
la crisi / the crisis	*le crisi* / the crises

§3.3 – 4 Spelling Peculiarities

When putting nouns that end in *-co, -go, -ca, -ga, -cio, -gio, -cia, -gia,* and *-io* into the plural, follow the patterns given below.

● Nouns ending in *-co* are pluralized as follows:

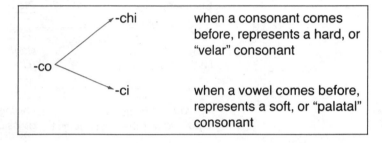

-chi	when a consonant comes before, represents a hard, or "velar" consonant
-co	
-ci	when a vowel comes before, represents a soft, or "palatal" consonant

EXAMPLES

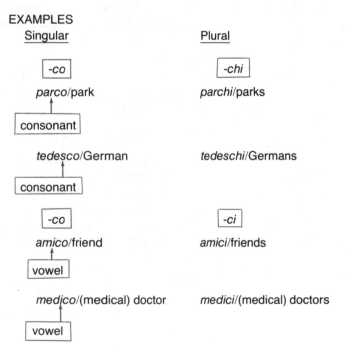

Singular	Plural
-co	-chi
parco/park	*parchi*/parks
consonant	
tedesco/German	*tedeschi*/Germans
consonant	
-co	-ci
amico/friend	*amici*/friends
vowel	
medico/(medical) doctor	*medici*/(medical) doctors
vowel	

EXCEPTIONS: *Porco* (pig), *fuoco* (fire), *fico* (fig), and *buco* (hole) have the following plural forms: por*ci*, fuo*chi*, fi*chi*, bu*chi*.

● Nouns ending in *-go* are pluralized as follows:

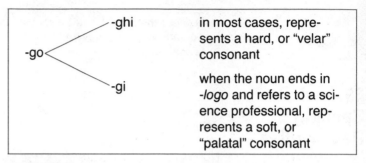

-ghi	in most cases, represents a hard, or "velar" consonant
-gi	when the noun ends in *-logo* and refers to a science professional, represents a soft, or "palatal" consonant

EXAMPLES

Singular	Plural

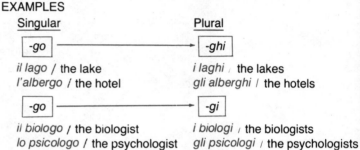

-go ─────────────► -ghi	
il lago / the lake	*i laghi* / the lakes
l'albergo / the hotel	*gli alberghi* / the hotels

-go ─────────────► -gi	
il biologo / the biologist	*i biologi* / the biologists
lo psicologo / the psychologist	*gli psicologi* / the psychologists

● But be careful! Not all nouns ending in *-logo* refer to scientists of some kind. In such cases, the *-go* becomes *-ghi* in the plural.

EXAMPLES

Singular	Plural
il catalogo / the catalog	*i cataloghi* / the catalogs
il dialogo / the dialogue	*i dialoghi* / the dialogues

● The above rules are to be considered only as guidelines.

● Nouns ending in *-ca* and *-ga* always retain the hard (velar) sound in the plural.

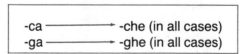

-ca ────────► -che (in all cases)
-ga ────────► -ghe (in all cases)

EXAMPLES

Singular	Plural
amica / (female) friend	*amiche* (female) friends
paga / pay (check)	*paghe* / pay (checks)

● Nouns ending in *-cio, -gio, -cia, -gia,* and *-io* are pluralized as follows:

If the *i* is stressed in the singular, then it is retained in the plural.

EXAMPLES

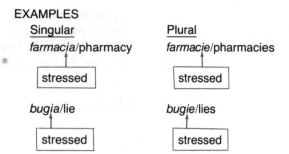

Singular	Plural
farmacia/pharmacy	*farmacie*/pharmacies
stressed	stressed
bugia/lie	*bugie*/lies
stressed	stressed

> If the *i* is not pronounced (as in English *social* and *Belgium*), it is not kept in the plural. In masculine nouns, this means that only one *i* is used.

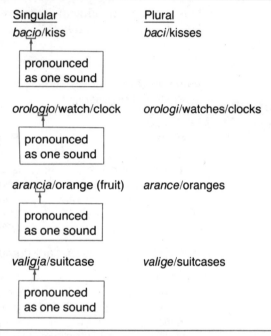

Singular	Plural
bacio/kiss	*baci*/kisses
pronounced as one sound	
orologio/watch/clock	*orologi*/watches/clocks
pronounced as one sound	
arancia/orange (fruit)	*arance*/oranges
pronounced as one sound	
valigia/suitcase	*valige*/suitcases
pronounced as one sound	

> EXCEPTION: *Camicia* (shirt) is pluralized as *camicie* although the second *i* is not stressed.

- A similar pattern applies to nouns ending in *-io*.

EXAMPLES

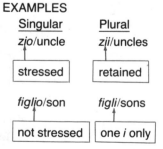

Singular	Plural
zio/uncle	*zii*/uncles
stressed	retained
figlio/son	*figli*/sons
not stressed	one *i* only

§3.3 – 5
Neuter Plurals

Like the English words "memorandum" and "compendium," which are pluralized by replacing the -*um* with -*a*, Italian also has a few plural forms in -*a*. These can be traced back to the Latin neuter forms that were pluralized in this way.

- Notice that in Italian, nouns pluralized in this way are masculine in the singular but feminine in the plural!

EXAMPLES

Singular	Plural
il dito / the finger	*le dita* / the fingers
il labbro / the lip	*le labbra* / the lips
il paio / the pair	*le paia* / the pairs
il miglio / the mile	*le miglia* / the miles

- There are not too many of these nouns, and most refer to parts of the human body.

§3.3 – 6
Miscellaneous Irregularities

Some nouns are abbreviations, and therefore do not change in the plural:

EXAMPLES

Singular	Plural
l'auto / the car	*le auto* / the cars
(from: *l'automobile*)	*le auto(mobili)*
il cinema / the movies	*i cinema* / the movie theaters
(from: *il cinematografo*)	*i cinema(tografi)*
la foto / the photo	*le foto* / the photos
(from: *la fotografia*)	*le foto(grafie)*

Some common nouns that are completely irregular are:

Singular	Plural
la mano / the hand (*f.*)	*le mani* the hands
l'uomo / the man (*m.*)	*gli uomini* the men
la radio / the radio (*f.*)	*le radio* / the radios

§3.4
TITLES

Be sure to drop the final -*e* of a masculine title when it comes before a name.

EXAMPLES

Masculine Title	Used Before a Name
il signore / the gentleman	*il signor Rossi* / Mr. Rossi
il professore / the professor	*il professor Verdi* / Professor Verdi
il dottore / the doctor	*il dottor Bianchi* / Dr. Bianchi
But retain the -*o*:	
l'avvocato/the lawyer	*l'avvocato Tozzi*/The lawyer Tozzi

Corresponding Feminine Titles

la signora / the lady	*la signora Rossi* / Mrs. Rossi
la professoressa / the professor	*la professoressa Verdi* / Professor Verdi
la dottoressa / the doctor	*la dottoressa Bianchi* / Dr. Bianchi
l'avvocatessa / the lawyer	*l'avvocatessa Tozzi* / the lawyer Tozzi

§3.5 NOUN SUFFIXES

In some cases, you can change the meaning of a noun by adding a suffix such as the following:

- *-ino/-ina* to add the meaning of "little" or "small" to the noun.

EXAMPLES
il ragazzo ⟶ *il ragazzino* / the little boy
la ragazza ⟶ *la ragazzina* / the little girl

- *-one/-ona* to add the meaning of "big" or "large" to the noun.

EXAMPLES
il ragazzo ⟶ *il ragazzone* / the big boy
la ragazza ⟶ *la ragazzona* / the big girl

- *-accio/-accia* to add the meaning of "bad" to the noun.

EXAMPLES
il ragazzo ⟶ *il ragazzaccio* / the bad boy
la ragazza ⟶ *la ragazzaccia* / the bad girl

- Be very careful when using these suffixes! They have many shades of meaning and can be used incorrectly. To avoid offending anyone, be absolutely sure of the meaning.

§3.6 COMPOUND NOUNS

Compound nouns are made up of two parts of speech:

Compound Noun

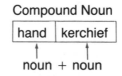

noun + noun

To form the plural of such nouns in Italian, observe the following guidelines:

- Most compound nouns are pluralized in the normal fashion (see §3.3–1).

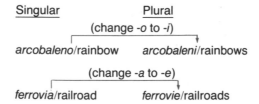

Singular   Plural
(change -o to -i)
arcobaleno/rainbow   *arcobaleni*/rainbows
(change -a to -e)
ferrovia/railroad   *ferrovie*/railroads

- Some change both parts of the compound noun.

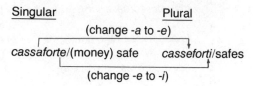

- Other compound nouns, especially those that contain a verb, do not change.

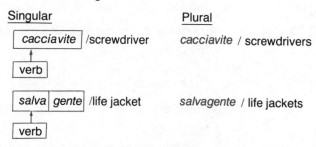

- As you can see, pluralizing compound nouns can be a complicated task. Like most Italians, check a dictionary to be sure you have pluralized the noun correctly.

§4.

Articles

Articles are words placed before nouns (or their modifying adjectives), in both English and Italian, that allow us to specify the nouns in some way.

Specific	Nonspecific
il libro / the book	*un libro* / a book

The article that allows us to speak of persons, objects, etc., in a specific way is called the *definite* article. The article that is used to designate nonspecific persons, objects, etc., is called the *indefinite* article.

Demonstratives will be included in this chapter, even though you will probably find them listed as adjectives in most grammars. They are included here because they too have the function of specifying a noun in some way. More precisely, demonstratives allow us to specify whether someone or something is relatively near or far.

Near	Far
questo libro / this book	*quel libro* / that book

Definite and indefinite articles, as well as demonstratives, vary according to the noun's gender, number, and initial sound.

The forms of the definite article are:

BEFORE MASCULINE NOUNS		
	Singular	**Plural**
Beginning with *z*, or *s* + consonant	lo	gli
Beginning with any vowel	l'	gli
Beginning with any other consonant	il	i
BEFORE FEMININE NOUNS		
Beginning with any consonant	la	le
Beginning with any vowel	l'	le

EXAMPLES

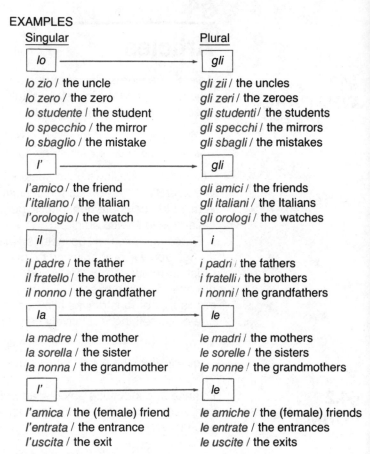

Singular	Plural
lo	*gli*
lo zio / the uncle	*gli zii* / the uncles
lo zero / the zero	*gli zeri* / the zeroes
lo studente / the student	*gli studenti* / the students
lo specchio / the mirror	*gli specchi* / the mirrors
lo sbaglio / the mistake	*gli sbagli* / the mistakes
l'	*gli*
l'amico / the friend	*gli amici* / the friends
l'italiano / the Italian	*gli italiani* / the Italians
l'orologio / the watch	*gli orologi* / the watches
il	*i*
il padre / the father	*i padri* / the fathers
il fratello / the brother	*i fratelli* / the brothers
il nonno / the grandfather	*i nonni* / the grandfathers
la	*le*
la madre / the mother	*le madri* / the mothers
la sorella / the sister	*le sorelle* / the sisters
la nonna / the grandmother	*le nonne* / the grandmothers
l'	*le*
l'amica / the (female) friend	*le amiche* / the (female) friends
l'entrata / the entrance	*le entrate* / the entrances
l'uscita / the exit	*le uscite* / the exits

- Be careful! With feminine nouns beginning with *z*, or *s* + consonant, you still use *la*: *la zia* (the aunt), *la scuola* (the school).

- The masculine form *lo* (plural *gli*) is also used in front of nouns beginning with *ps* or *gn* (and a few other unusual initial sounds).

EXAMPLES

lo psicologo / the psychologist	*gli psicologi* / the psychologists
lo gnocco / the dumpling	*gli gnocchi* / the dumplings

- Note, however, that there are only a few such nouns.

- Be careful! When an adjective precedes the noun, you will have to adjust the definite article according to its beginning sound.

la zia/the aunt

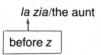

before *z*

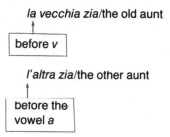

la vecchia zia/the old aunt

before *v*

l'altra zia/the other aunt

before the vowel *a*

The forms of the indefinite article in the singular are as follows. Pluralization of the indefinite article is discussed in Chapter 5.

§4.2 – 2
The Indefinite Article (Italian equivalent of "a/an")

BEFORE MASCULINE NOUNS	
Beginning with *z* or *s* + consonant ⟶	uno
Beginning with any other sound (consonant or vowel) ⟶	un
BEFORE FEMININE NOUNS	
Beginning with any consonant ⟶	una
Beginning with any vowel ⟶	un'

- Note that the apostrophe (*un'*) is used only when the indefinite article is in front of a feminine noun beginning with a vowel.

- As in the case of the definite article (see §4.2–1), the form *uno* also is used in front of nouns beginning with *ps* and *gn*.

EXAMPLES

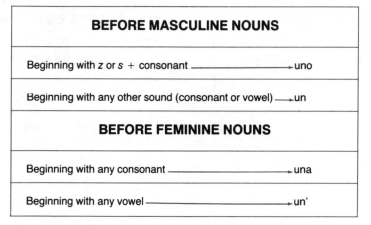

uno ⟶	*un*
uno zio / an uncle	*un piede* / a foot
uno sbaglio / a mistake	*un braccio* / an arm
uno psicologo / a psychologist	*un occhio* / an eye
uno gnocco / a dumpling	*un orecchio* / an ear

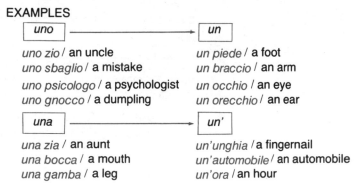

una ⟶	*un'*
una zia / an aunt	*un'unghia* / a fingernail
una bocca / a mouth	*un'automobile* / an automobile
una gamba / a leg	*un'ora* / an hour

- Don't forget! When an adjective precedes the noun, you will have to adjust the indefinite article according to the beginning sound.

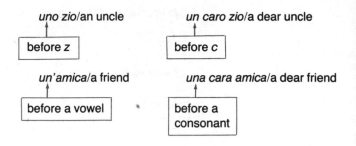

§4.2 – 3 The Demonstratives ("this/these, that/those" in Italian)

The forms of the demonstrative are:

DEMONSTRATIVE INDICATING "NEARNESS"	
Before Masculine Nouns	
Singular	Plural
quest o	quest i
Before Feminine Nouns	
quest a	quest e

EXAMPLES

questo	⟶	questi

questo sbaglio / this mistake
questo giornale / this newspaper
questo esercizio / this exercise

questi sbagli / these mistakes
questi giornali / these newspapers
questi esercizi / these exercises

questa	⟶	queste

questa stanza / this room
questa ora / this hour

queste stanze / these rooms
queste ore / these hours

- The form *quest'* is often used before singular nouns (or modifying adjectives) beginning with a vowel.

Singular	Plural
questo	
quest'	questi

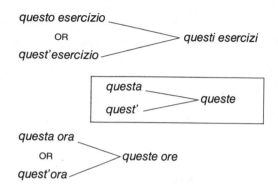

questo esercizio
OR → questi esercizi
quest'esercizio

questa
quest' → queste

questa ora
OR → queste ore
quest'ora

DEMONSTRATIVE INDICATING "FARTHER AWAY"		
Before Masculine Nouns		
	Singular	Plural
Beginning with *z* or *s* + consonant	quello	
Beginning with any vowel	quell'	quegli
Beginning with any other consonant	quel ——— quei	
Before Feminine Nouns		
Beginning with any consonant	quella	
Beginning with any vowel	quell'	quelle

As with articles (see §4.2–1 and §4.2–2), the form *quello* (plural *quegli*) is also used before those few nouns beginning with *ps* and *gn*.

EXAMPLES

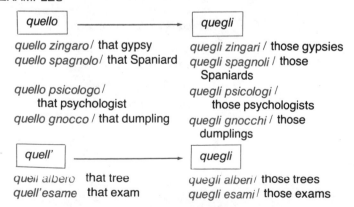

quello	→	quegli

quello zingaro/ that gypsy — *quegli zingari* / those gypsies
quello spagnolo/ that Spaniard — *quegli spagnoli* / those Spaniards
quello psicologo/ that psychologist — *quegli psicologi* / those psychologists
quello gnocco / that dumpling — *quegli gnocchi* / those dumplings

quell'	→	quegli

quell'albero that tree — *quegli alberi*/ those trees
quell'esame that exam — *quegli esami*/ those exams

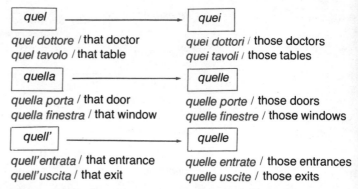

quel dottore / that doctor
quel tavolo / that table

quei dottori / those doctors
quei tavoli / those tables

quella porta / that door
quella finestra / that window

quelle porte / those doors
quelle finestre / those windows

quell'entrata / that entrance
quell'uscita / that exit

quelle entrate / those entrances
quelle uscite / those exits

- Be careful! As with articles, when an adjective precedes a noun, you will have to change the demonstrative according to the adjective's initial sound.

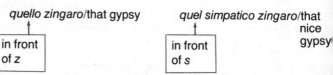

- If you look very closely, you will see that this demonstrative is exactly like the definite article.

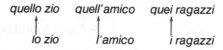

**§4.3
USES**

Articles and demonstratives are used in ways similar to English. Note, however, the following differences:

- In Italian the definite article is used in front of noncount nouns (see §3.1) used as subjects (normally at the start of a sentence).

EXAMPLES

L'acqua è un liquido. Water is a liquid.
Il cibo è necessario per vivere. / Food is necessary to live.
La pazienza è una virtù. / Patience is a virtue.

- This is true even in the case of count nouns used in the plural to express generalizations.

EXAMPLES

Gli italiani sono simpatici. / Italians are nice.
I libri ci aiutano a capire. / Books help us understand.

- As a guideline, just remember that you *cannot* start an Italian sentence with a noun without its article.

- Needless to say, you do not use an indefinite article with noncount nouns ("a hunger," "a water").

- The definite article is used in front of geographical names (continents, countries, states, rivers, islands, mountains, etc.), *except* cities.

  EXAMPLES

l'Italia / Italy	*la Sicilia* / Sicily
gli Stati Uniti / the United States	*il Tevere* / the Tiber
la California / California	*il Mediterraneo* / the Mediterranean
il Belgio / Belgium	*le Alpi* / the Alps
	il Piemonte / Piedmont

  But:

  Roma / Rome
  Washington / Washington
  Parigi / Paris

- Notice that the gender of a geographical noun is usually determined in the usual fashion by its ending (see §3.2). If you are in doubt, consult a dictionary.

- The definite article is usually dropped after the preposition *in* and before an unmodified geographical noun.

  EXAMPLES

  Vado in Italia. / I'm going to Italy.
  Abito in Francia. / I live in France.

  But when the noun is modified:

  Vado nell'Italia centrale. / I'm going to central Italy.
  Abito nella Francia meridionale. / I live in southern France.

- The definite article is used with *dates.*

  EXAMPLES

  Il 1492 è un anno importante. / 1492 is an important year.
  Oggi è il tre novembre. / Today is November third.

  (Note that the *il* form is used).

- The definite article is commonly used in place of possessive adjectives (see §6.4–3) when referring to family members (singular only), parts of the body, and clothing.

  Oggi vado in centro con la zia. / Today I'm going downtown with my aunt.
  Mi fa male la gamba. / My leg hurts.
  Mario non si mette mai la giacca. / Mario never puts his jacket on.

- The definite article is used with the days of the week to indicate an habitual action.

EXAMPLES
Il lunedì gioco a tennis. / On Mondays I play tennis.
La domenica vado in chiesa. / On Sundays I go to church.

- Note that the days of the week, except Sunday, are masculine.

- The definite article is not used when a specific day is intended.

Il lunedì gioco a tennis, ma lunedì vado via. / On Mondays I play tennis, but Monday I'm going away.

- The definite article is used with titles, unless you are speaking *directly* to the person mentioned.

EXAMPLES

Speaking about	Speaking to
Il dottor Verdi è italiano. / Dr. Verdi is Italian.	*Buon giorno, dottor Verdi.* Hello, Dr. Verdi.
La professoressa Bianchi è molto intelligente. / Professor Bianchi is very intelligent.	*Professoressa Bianchi, dove abita?* / Professor Bianchi, where do you live?

- A similar pattern occurs in English when the name of the person is not mentioned.

Il dottore è malato. / The doctor is ill.
Dottore, è malato? / Doctor, are you ill?

- The definite article is used before names of languages and school subjects (except with the verb *parlare*).

EXAMPLES
Impariamo lo spagnolo. / We are learning Spanish.
Studio la matematica. / I am studying mathematics.

- It is dropped with the prepositions *di* and *in*.

EXAMPLES
Ecco il libro di spagnolo. / Here is the Spanish book.
Sono bravo in matematica. / I'm good in math.

- The definite article is used with *scorso* (last) and *prossimo* (next) in time expressions.

EXAMPLES
la settimana scorsa / last week
il mese prossimo / next month

- Note that the definite article is not used in many common expressions, such as:

  a destra / to the right
  a sinistra / to the left
  a casa / at home

- The indefinite article also translates the number "one:"
  un'arancia = an orange OR one orange

- The indefinite article is not used in exclamations starting with *Che . . . !*

  EXAMPLES
  Che film! / What a film!
  Che bel vestito! / What a beautiful dress!

- Finally, remember to repeat the articles and demonstratives before every noun.

  un ragazzo e una ragazza / a boy and girl
  il ragazzo e la ragazza / the boy and girl
  questo ragazzo e questa ragazza / this boy and girl
  quel ragazzo e quella ragazza / that boy and girl

§5.

Partitives

§5.1
WHAT ARE
PARTITIVES?

Partitives are words placed before Italian nouns that express the notion of "some" or "any," i.e., they refer to a *part* of something.

    dell'acqua / some water   *degli esami* / some tests

§5.2
WITH COUNT
NOUNS

Before count nouns (see §3.1), the partitive can be considered the plural of the indefinite article (see §4.2–2). The most commonly used partitive in this case is the preposition *di* + the plural forms of the definite article (as they occur normally in front of nouns).

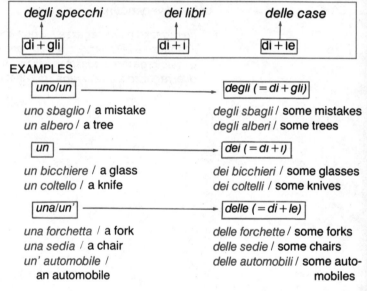

EXAMPLES

| uno/un | → | degli (= di + gli) |

uno sbaglio / a mistake   *degli sbagli* / some mistakes
un albero / a tree   *degli alberi* / some trees

| un | → | dei (= di + i) |

un bicchiere / a glass   *dei bicchieri* / some glasses
un coltello / a knife   *dei coltelli* / some knives

| una/un' | → | delle (= di + le) |

una forchetta / a fork   *delle forchette* / some forks
una sedia / a chair   *delle sedie* / some chairs
un' automobile /   *delle automobili* / some auto-
    an automobile   mobiles

- The partitive pronouns *alcuni* (m.) and *alcune* (f.) are often used to express the idea of "some." They are used only in the plural.

> *degli* zii OR *alcuni* zii
> *dei* bicchieri OR *alcuni* bicchieri
> *delle* forchette OR *alcune* forchette
> *delle* amiche OR *alcune* amiche (f.)

- Actually, these two types can be used together in expressions such as:

- A third type of partitive used with count nouns is the invariable pronoun *qualche*. But be careful with this one! It must be followed by a *singular* noun, even though the meaning is plural!

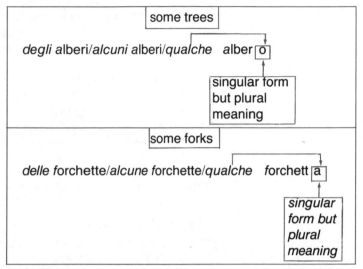

- *Qualche* or *alcuni/alcune* are often used at the start of sentences, rather than the more awkward *degli/dei/delle* forms. Once again, be careful with *qualche:* it requires a *singular* verb!

- In current Italian, it is not unusual to find that the partitive is omitted (when the noun is not the first word in a sentence).

EXAMPLES

Voglio *della* carne. OR Voglio carne. (I want [some] meat.)
Mangio *degli* spaghetti. OR Mangio spaghetti. (I'm eating [some] spaghetti.)

- In negative sentences, the partitive (translated as "any") is omitted.

EXAMPLES

Affirmative Sentence	Negative Sentence
Ho dei biglietti. / I have some tickets.	*Non ho biglietti.* / I don't have any tickets.
Voglio delle paste. / I want some pastries.	*Non voglio paste.* / I don't want any pastries.

- The partitive can also be rendered by *non . . . nessuno.* Think of *nessuno* as being made up of "ness" + *indefinite article.*

---

nessuno corresponds to *uno: uno studente/nessuno studente*
nessun corresponds to *un: un biglietto/nessun biglietto*
nessuna corresponds to *una: una signora/nessuna signora*
nessun' corresponds to *un': un'automobile/nessun' automobile*

- This means that after the forms of *nessuno* the noun is always in the singular, even though the meaning is plural.

EXAMPLES

Affirmative Sentence	Negative Sentence
Carlo compra degli specchi. / Charles buys some mirrors.	*Carlo non compra nessuno specchio.* / Charles does not buy any mirrors.
Carla compra delle caramelle. / Carla buys some candies.	*Carla non compra nessuna caramella.* / Carla does not buy any candies.

§5.3 WITH NON-COUNT NOUNS

With noncount nouns (see §3.1), the partitive is rendered by *di* + the singular forms of the definite article (according to the noun), or by the expression *un po' di* ("a bit of").

EXAMPLES

Voglio del pane. OR *Voglio un po' di pane.*/I want some bread.
$$\boxed{di + il}$$

Lui vuole dello zucchero. OR *Lui vuole un po' di zucchero.*/ He wants some sugar.
$$\boxed{di + lo}$$

Maria mangia dell'insalata. OR *Maria mangia un po' di insalata.*/ Mary eats some salad.
$$\boxed{di + l'}$$

Preferisco mangiare della carne. OR *Preferisco mangiare un po' di carne.*/I prefer to eat some meat.
$$\boxed{di + la}$$

§5.4
SUMMARY

The following chart summarizes the various partitive forms:

PARTITIVES WITH COUNT NOUNS	
Singular Forms of the Indefinite Article	**Corresponding Plural Forms**
uno/un — ↑ masculine, in front of a vowel	degli alcuni qualche + singular noun
un — ↑ masculine, in front of all consonants except *z*, and *s* + consonant	dei alcuni qualche + singular noun
una/un' —	delle alcune qualche + singular noun
PARTITIVES WITH NONCOUNT NOUNS	
Masculine Forms	**Equivalent**
del (= di + il) dell' (= di + l') dello (= di + lo)	un po' di
Feminine Forms	
della (= di + la) dell' (= di + l')	un po' di

- Remember! As in the case of articles and demonstratives (see Chapter 4), you will have to change the partitive forms when an adjective precedes the noun.

  degli zii BUT *dei simpatici zii*

§6.

Adjectives

§6.1
WHAT ARE
ADJECTIVES?

Adjectives are words that modify, or describe, nouns. They are placed before or after the noun they modify.

È una casa nuova. / It's a new house.
È il mio libro. / It's my book.

§6.2
AGREEMENT

Adjectives must agree with the nouns they modify. This means that an adjective must correspond in gender and number with the noun. Thus, the ending of an adjective depends on whether the noun is masculine or feminine, singular or plural.

There are two types of adjectives according to their endings.

● Adjectives that end in -*o* (masculine singular) have the following set of endings that agree with the noun:

	Singular	Plural
Masculine	-o	-i
Feminine	-a	-e

EXAMPLES

Singular

l'uomo alt o / the tall man

il figlio alt o / the tall son

la donna alt a / the tall woman

la madre alt a / the tall mother

Plural

gli uomini alt i /the tall men

i figli alt i /the tall sons

le donne alt e /the tall women

le madri alt e /the tall mothers

● Adjectives that end in -*e* in the singular have two endings, according to whether they modify a singular noun (masculine or feminine) or plural noun (masculine or feminine):

	Singular	Plural
Masculine or Feminine	-e	-i

EXAMPLES

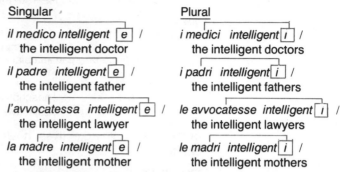

Singular

il medico intelligent e / the intelligent doctor

il padre intelligent e / the intelligent father

l'avvocatessa intelligent e / the intelligent lawyer

la madre intelligent e / the intelligent mother

Plural

i medici intelligent i / the intelligent doctors

i padri intelligent i / the intelligent fathers

le avvocatesse intelligent i / the intelligent lawyers

le madri intelligent i / the intelligent mothers

- A few adjectives are invariable, that is, their ending never changes. The most common are the adjectives of color: *marrone* (brown), *arancione* (orange), *viola* (violet, purple), *rosa* (pink), and *blu* (dark blue).

EXAMPLES

Singular	Plural
il vestito marrone / the brown suit	*i vestiti marrone* / the brown suits
la giacca marrone / the brown jacket	*le giacche marrone* / the brown jackets

- When two nouns are modified, the adjective is always in the plural. If the two nouns are feminine, then use a feminine plural ending. If the two nouns are both masculine, or of mixed gender, then use the masculine plural ending.

EXAMPLES

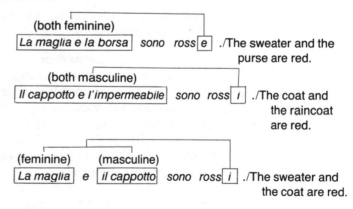

(both feminine)
La maglia e la borsa sono ross e ./The sweater and the purse are red.

(both masculine)
Il cappotto e l'impermeabile sono ross i ./The coat and the raincoat are red.

(feminine)   (masculine)
La maglia e il cappotto sono ross i ./The sweater and the coat are red.

§6.3 POSITION

Interrogative (see §6.4–2) and possessive (see §6.4–3) adjectives *precede* the noun they modify, whereas descriptive adjectives (see §6.4–1) generally *follow* the noun.

Quante scarpe hai comprato?/How many shoes did you buy?

interrogative adjective

I tuoi pantaloni sono lunghi./Your pants are long.

possessive
adjective

Ieri ho comprato una camicia bianca./Yesterday I bought a
white shirt.

descriptive
adjective

Some descriptive adjectives, however, can be used before
or after.

EXAMPLES

È una bella camicia.   OR   *È una camicia bella.*/It's a
beautiful shirt.

Maria è una ragazza simpatica. OR *Maria è una simpatica ragazza.*/
Mary is a nice girl.

- You will eventually learn which descriptive adjectives can
  come before through practice and use.

- Be careful! As discussed in Chapter 4, you will have to
  change the form of the article when you put the adjective
  before.

  lo zio simpatico BUT *il simpatico zio*

  before *z*   before *s*

- Some common descriptive adjectives that can come before
  or after a noun are:

bello/	*cattivo*/bad	*piccolo*/small, little
beautiful	*giovane*/young	*povero*/poor
brutto/ugly	*grande*/big, large	*simpatico*/nice,
buono/good	*nuovo*/new	charming
caro/dear		*vecchio*/old

- But be careful! A few of these adjectives change meaning
  according to their position.

  EXAMPLES
  È un ragazzo povero. = He is a poor (not wealthy) boy.
  È un povero ragazzo. = He is a poor (deserving of pity) boy.

  È un amico vecchio. = He is an old (in age) friend.
  È un vecchio amico. = He is an old (for many years) friend.

- As always, when you are unsure of the meaning and use of
  an adjective, check a dictionary.

Descriptive adjectives can also be separated from the noun they modify by what is called a *linking* verb. The most common linking verbs are *essere* (to be), *sembrare* (to seem), and *diventare* (to become).

EXAMPLES

Quella casa è nuov⟦a⟧ ./That house is new.

Quell'uomo sembra giovan⟦e⟧ ./That man seems young.

- Adjectives used in this way are known as *predicate adjectives* because they occur in the predicate slot, *after* the verb that links them to the noun they modify.

One final word about the position of descriptive adjectives! When these adjectives are accompanied by an adverb, another adjective, or some other part of speech, they must *follow* the noun.

EXAMPLES

È un ⟦simpatico⟧ *ragazzo.*/He is a pleasant boy.

BUT

È un ragazzo ⟦molto simpatico.⟧ /He is a very pleasant boy.

È un ragazzo ⟦simpatico e buono.⟧ /He is a pleasant and good boy.

§6.4 TYPES

The four most common types of adjectives are *demonstrative, descriptive, interrogative,* and *possessive.* Demonstrative adjectives have already been discussed in §4.2–3.

§6.4 – 1 Descriptive

Descriptive adjectives specify a quality of the noun they modify. They make up the largest group of adjectives. As already discussed (see §6.2), descriptive adjectives generally follow the noun.

È un esame difficile./It's a difficult test.

Of the adjectives that can come *before* the noun, *buono* (good), *bello* (beautiful), *santo* (saint[ly]), and *grande* (big, large), change in form when they are placed before.

- *Buono* changes exactly like the indefinite article (see §4.2–2).

BEFORE MASCULINE NOUNS		
	Singular	**Plural**
Beginning with z, s + consonant, *ps, gn*	*buono*	
Beginning with any other sound (vowel or consonant)	*buon*	*buoni*
BEFORE FEMININE NOUNS		
Beginning with any consonant	buona	
Beginning with any vowel	buon'	buone

- When it is placed after the noun, *buono* is a normal adjective ending in *-o* (see §6.2).

  EXAMPLES

  Singular:

  un buono zio OR *uno zio buon* o   (a good uncle)

  un buon libro OR *un libro buon* o   (a good book)

  un buon amico OR *un amico buon* o   (a good friend)

  una buona macchina OR *una macchina buon* a   (a good car)

  una buon'amica OR *un'amica buon* a   (a good friend)

  Plural:

  dei buoni zii OR *degli zii buon* i   ([some] good uncles)

  dei buoni amici OR *degli amici buon* i   ([some] good friends)

  delle buone macchine OR *delle macchine buon* e   ([some] good cars)

  delle buone amiche OR *delle amiche buon* e   ([some] good friends)

- Notice that the apostrophe is used only with the feminine form (*buon'*), as is the case for the indefinite article (see §4.2–2).

- When referring to people, *buono* means "good," in the sense of "good in nature." If "good at doing something" is intended, then you must use the adjective *bravo*.

  È un buon ragazzo. = He is a good (natured) boy
  È un bravo studente. = He is a good student. (i.e., He is good at being a student.)

- *Bello* changes exactly like the definite article (see §4.2–1) and the demonstrative *quello* (see §4.2–3).

BEFORE MASCULINE NOUNS		
	Singular	**Plural**
Beginning with *z, s* + consonant, *ps, gn*	bello	begli
Beginning with any vowel	bell'	begli
Beginning with any other consonant	bel	bei
BEFORE FEMININE NOUNS		
Beginning with any consonant	bella	belle
Beginning with any vowel	bell'	belle

- If placed after the noun, *bello* is a normal adjective ending in *-o* (see §6.2).

  EXAMPLES

  Singular:

  un bello sport OR *uno sport bell* $\boxed{o}$ (a beautiful sport)
  un bell'orologio OR *un orologio bell* $\boxed{o}$ (a beautiful watch)
  un bel fiore OR *un fiore bell* $\boxed{o}$ (a beautiful flower)
  una bella donna OR *una donna bell* $\boxed{a}$ (a beautiful woman)
  una bell'automobile OR *un'automobile bell* $\boxed{a}$ (a beautiful automobile)

  Plural:

  dei begli sport OR *degli sport bell* $\boxed{i}$ ([some] beautiful sports)
  dei begli orologi OR *degli orologi bell* $\boxed{i}$ ([some] beautiful watches)
  dei bei fiori OR *dei fiori bell* $\boxed{i}$ ([some] beautiful flowers)
  delle belle automobili OR *delle automobili bell* $\boxed{e}$ ([some] beautiful automobiles)

- *Santo* has the following forms when placed before the noun.

BEFORE MASCULINE NOUNS		
	Singular	**Plural**
Beginning with *z, s* + consonant, *ps, gn*	santo	santi
Beginning with any vowel	sant'	santi
Beginning with any other consonant	san	santi

BEFORE FEMININE NOUNS		
	Singular	**Plural**
Beginning with any consonant	santa	sante
Beginning with any vowel	sant'	sante

EXAMPLES

Singular	*Plural*
Santo Stefano	*i santi Stefano, Antonio, e Pietro* (Saints Stephen, Anthony, and Peter)
Sant'Antonio	
San Pietro	
Santa Caterina	*le sante Caterina e Anna* (Saints Catherine and Anne)
Sant'Anna	

- *Grande* has the optional forms *gran* (before a masculine singular noun beginning with any consonant except *z, s +* consonant, *ps*, and *gn*), and *grand'* before any singular noun beginning with a vowel. Otherwise, it is a normal adjective ending in *-e* (see 6.2).

EXAMPLES
un gran film (a great film) OR *un grande film*
un grand'amico (a great friend) OR *un grande amico*

- Note that in the preceding examples, the articles and partitives are changed according to the initial sound of the word they precede—noun or adjective (see §4.2–1, §4.2–2, §4.2–3).

Those adjectives ending in *-co, -go, -cio*, and *-gio* have the same spelling patterns when pluralized as the nouns ending in these sounds (see §3.3–4).

EXAMPLES

Singular	*Plural*
un uomo simpatico / a pleasant man	*degli uomini simpatici* / (some) nice men
una strada lunga / a long street	*delle strade lunghe* / (some) long streets
un vestito grigio / a gray suit	*dei vestiti grigi* / (some) gray suits

§6.4 – 2
Interrogative

Interrogative adjectives allow us to ask questions about nouns.

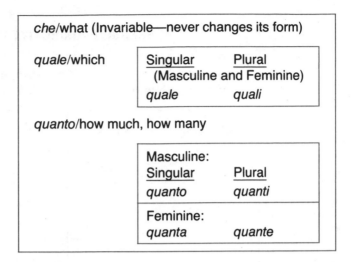

che/what (Invariable—never changes its form)

quale/which

Singular	Plural
(Masculine and Feminine)	
quale	*quali*

quanto/how much, how many

Masculine:	
Singular	Plural
quanto	*quanti*
Feminine:	
quanta	*quante*

These adjectives always come before the noun.

EXAMPLES

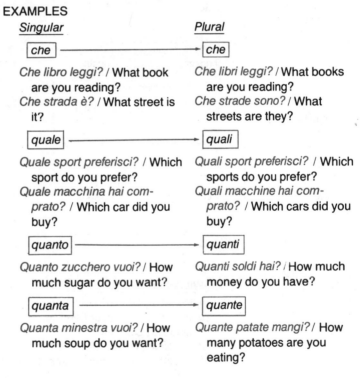

Singular	Plural
che ⟶	che
Che libro leggi? / What book are you reading?	*Che libri leggi?* / What books are you reading?
Che strada è? / What street is it?	*Che strade sono?* / What streets are they?
quale ⟶	quali
Quale sport preferisci? / Which sport do you prefer?	*Quali sport preferisci?* / Which sports do you prefer?
Quale macchina hai comprato? / Which car did you buy?	*Quali macchine hai comprato?* / Which cars did you buy?
quanto ⟶	quanti
Quanto zucchero vuoi? / How much sugar do you want?	*Quanti soldi hai?* / How much money do you have?
quanta ⟶	quante
Quanta minestra vuoi? / How much soup do you want?	*Quante patate mangi?* / How many potatoes are you eating?

§6.4 – 3 Possessive

Possessive adjectives allow us to indicate ownership of, or relationship to, a noun.

il mio libro / my book (ownership of)
le nostre amiche / our (female) friends (relationship to)

Like all adjectives, possessive adjectives agree in number and gender with the noun they modify.

	POSSESSIVE ADJECTIVE FORMS			
	Before Masculine Nouns		**Before Feminine Nouns**	
	Singular	**Plural**	**Singular**	**Plural**
my	il mio	i miei	la mia	le mie
your (familiar singular)	il tuo	i tuoi	la tua	le tue
his, her, its	il suo	i suoi	la sua	le sue
your (polite singular)	il Suo	i Suoi	la Sua	le Sue
our	il nostro	i nostri	la nostra	le nostre
your (familiar plural)	il vostro	i vostri	la vostra	le vostre
their	il loro	i loro	la loro	le loro
your (polite plural)	il Loro	i Loro	la Loro	le Loro

EXAMPLES

With Singular Nouns

il mio cappotto / my coat
la tua bicicletta / your (familiar, singular) bicycles
il suo biglietto / his, her ticket
la nostra camera / our bedroom

il vostro passaporto / your (familiar, plural) passport
la loro casa / their house
il Suo indirizzo / your (polite, singular) address
il Loro lavoro / your (polite, plural) job

With Plural Nouns

i miei cappotti / my coats
le tue biciclette / your bicycles

il suoi biglietti / his, her tickets
le nostre camere / our bedrooms

i vostri passaporti /your passports
le loro case / their houses
i Suoi indirizzi / your addresses

i Loro lavori / your jobs

- As you can see, possessives are adjectives that come before the noun and agree with it in gender and number.

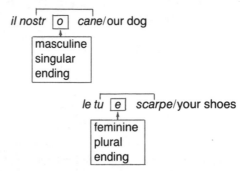

il nostr o *cane*/our dog

masculine
singular
ending

le tu e *scarpe*/your shoes

feminine
plural
ending

- The only invariable form is *loro*: it *never* changes.

- Notice that the definite article (in its appropriate form) is part of the possessive adjective. It is, however, dropped for all forms except *loro* when the noun modified has the following characteristics.

It is a kinship noun (i.e, it refers to family members or relatives).
It is singular.
It is unmodified (i.e., it is not accompanied by another adjective, or altered by a suffix — §3.5).

used when kinship noun is plural

tuo cugino / your cousin   *i tuoi cugini* / your cousins
mia sorella / my sister   BUT *le mie sorelle* / my sisters
nostro fratello / our brother   *i nostri fratelli* / our brothers

used when kinship noun is modified

il tuo nonno americano / your American grandfather
la mia sorellina / my little sister (see §3.5)
la nostra nonna italiana / our Italian grandmother

- As already mentioned, the article is always retained with *loro*.

  il loro figlio / their son
  la loro figlia / their daughter
  il loro fratello / their brother

- The only kinship nouns to which the above rules do not apply are *mamma* (mom) and *papà (babbo)* (dad).

  mia madre / my mother   *la mia mamma* / my mom
  tuo padre / your father   BUT *il tuo papà* / your dad

- Notice that both "his" and "her" are expressed by the same possessive (which takes on the appropriate form before the noun).

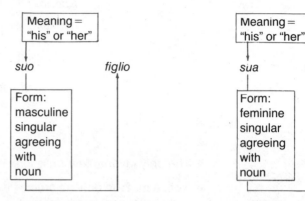

- As a handy guideline, make the possessive adjective agree with the noun first. Then worry about what it means in English. Otherwise, you will confuse its form with its meaning!

- Notice that "your" has both *familiar* and *polite* forms. More will be said about this distinction in the next chapter (see §7.3–1). As these terms imply, you use familiar forms with the people you know well and with whom you are on familiar terms; otherwise you use the polite forms.

- Note also that the polite forms are identical to the "his, her" forms in the singular, and the "their" forms in the plural. To keep the two types distinct in writing, the polite forms are often capitalized, as has been done here. But this is *not* an obligatory rule.

- Thus, when you see or hear these forms, you will have to figure out what they mean from the context.

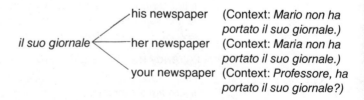

First context: Mario didn't bring his newspaper.
Second context: Mary didn't bring her newspaper.
Third context: Professor, did you bring your newspaper?

- In current Italian, it is not unusual to find only the *vostro* forms used as the plural of both the familiar and polite singular forms.

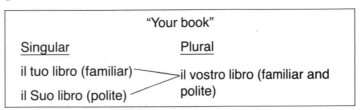

"Your book"

Singular	Plural
il tuo libro (familiar)	il vostro libro (familiar and
il Suo libro (polite)	polite)

- The use of *Loro* as the polite plural possessive is restricted to *very* formal situations (see §7.3–1).

- The possessive adjective can be put after the noun for emphasis.

    È il mio cane./It's my dog.   *È il cane mio!*/It's my dog!

- If the possessive adjective is preceded by the indefinite article, it expresses the idea "of mine," "of yours," etc.

    EXAMPLES
    un mio zio / an uncle of mine
    una sua amica / a friend of his, hers

- To express "own," use the adjective *proprio.*

    il mio proprio cane / my own dog
    la (sua) propria chiave / his, her own key

- Notice, finally, that the article is dropped when speaking directly to someor .

    Figlio mio, che fai? / My son, what are you doing?

§6.4 – 4
Other
Common
Adjectives

There are a few other adjectives you should know. Some of these are known formally as *indefinite* adjectives. The most common are:

Invariable	Like regular adjectives ending in -o
abbastanza/enough	*altro*/other
assai/quite, enough	*certo*/certain
ogni/each, every	*molto*/much, many, a lot
qualsiasi/whichever, any	*poco*/little, few
qualunque/ whichever, any	*parecchio*/several, a lot
	tanto/much, many, a lot
	troppo/too much
	stesso/the same
	ultimo/last
	tutto/all

EXAMPLES

Invariable

Non ho abbastanza soldi. / I do not have enough money.
Lui mangia assai carne. / He eats quite a lot of meat.
Ogni mattina leggiamo il giornale. / Every morning we read the newspaper.
In Italia puoi andare a qualsiasi (qualunque) ristorante /
   In Italy you can go to any restaurant.

Variable

Chi è l'altra ragazza? / Who is the other girl?
Conosco un certo signore che si chiama Roberto. / I know a certain gentleman (who is) named Robert.
Ieri ho mangiato molti (tanti) dolci. /
   Yesterday I ate a lot of sweets.
Ci sono poche studentesse in questa classe. / There are few female students in this class.
Parecchi turisti visitano Venezia. / Several (a lot of) tourists visit Venice.
Abbiamo mangiato troppo gelato. / We ate too much ice cream.
Questi sono gli stessi libri.   These are the same books.
Questa è l'ultima volta che ti telefonerò. / This is the last time I'm going to call you.

- The adjectives *ogni, qualsiasi*, and *qualunque* are always followed by a *singular* noun.

- *Alcuni, alcune* (some), *qualche* (some), and *nessuno* (any) are technically indefinite adjectives. However, they are used primarily with a partitive function (see §5.2).

- Notice that *tutto* is separated from the noun by the definite article.

EXAMPLES

Lei ha mangiato tutto il riso. / She ate all the rice.
Mario ha mangiato tutta la minestra. / Mario ate all the soup.

- *Molto, tanto, poco,* and *troppo* are also used as adverbs, in which case there is no agreement. More will be said about this in Chapter 9 (see §9.3).

§6.5 COMPARISON OF ADJECTIVES

We make a comparison of descriptive adjectives (see §6.4–1) when we want to indicate that some quality has a relatively equal, greater, or lesser degree of the quality.
The three degrees of comparison are: *positive, comparative,* and *superlative*.

> For the positive degree use either *così . . . come* or
> *tanto . . . quanto.*

EXAMPLES

Paola è così felice come sua sorella. / Paula is as happy as her
sister.

Quei ragazzi sono tanto noiosi quanto gli altri. / Those boys are
as boring as
the others.

- The first words (*così* or *tanto*) are optional.
Paola è felice come sua sorella.
Quei ragazzi sono noiosi quanto gli altri.

> For the comparative degree simply use *più* (more) or
> *meno* (less), as the case may be.

EXAMPLES

Maria è più studiosa di sua sorella. / Mary is more studious than
her sister.

Maria è meno alta di suo fratello. / Mary is shorter than her
brother.

Quei ragazzi sono più generosi degli altri. /
Those boys are more generous than the others.

Quei ragazzi sono meno intelligenti di quelle ragazze. / Those
boys are less intelligent than those girls.

> For the *superlative degree* use the definite article (in
> its proper form, of course!) followed by *più* or *meno*, as
> the case may be.

EXAMPLES

Maria è la più studiosa della sua classe. / Mary is the most studious in her class.

Quel ragazzo è il più simpatico della famiglia. / That boy is the
nicest in his
family.

Le patate sono le meno costose. / Potatoes are the least
expensive.

- In superlative constructions, the definite article is not
repeated if it is already in front of a noun.

Maria è la ragazza più studiosa della classe. / Mary is the most
studious girl in
the class.

Lui è il ragazzo meno intelligente della classe. / He is the least
intelligent boy
in the class.

- Notice that "in the" is rendered by *di* + definite article (if needed).

  Gina è la più elegante della scuola./Gina is the most elegant in the school.

  | di + la |

  Lui è il meno generoso dei miei amici./He is the least generous of my friends.

  | di + i |

  È il ristorante più caro di Roma./It's the most expensive restaurant in Rome.

- In comparative constructions, the word "than" is rendered in one of two ways according to the following patterns:

  | If two nouns are compared by one adjective, use *di*. |

  EXAMPLES

  | only adjective |

  Giovanni è più alto di Pietro./John is taller than Peter.

  | two nouns |

  | only adjective |

  Questo signore è meno elegante dell'altro signore./

  | two nouns |

  This gentleman is less elegant than the other gentleman.

  | If one noun and two adjectives modifying the same noun are involved, then use *che*. |

  | only noun |

  Giovanni è più elegante che bello./John is more elegant than handsome.

  | two adjectives |

  | only noun |

  Questa ragazza è più simpatica che bella./This girl is more friendly than beautiful.

  | two adjectives |

- If "than what" (= "than that which") is needed, then use *di quello che/di quel che/di ciò che*.

$$\textit{È più intelligente di} \begin{cases} \textit{quello} \\ \textit{quel che crediamo.} \\ \textit{ciò} \end{cases} \text{/ He is more intelligent than we believe.}$$

Some adjectives have both regular and irregular comparative and superlative forms. The most commonly used ones are:

Adjective	Comparative	Superlative
buono/good	più buono OR migliore*	il più buono OR il migliore
cattivo/bad	più cattivo OR peggiore*	il più cattivo OR il peggiore
grande/big, large	più grande OR maggiore	il più grande OR il maggiore
piccolo/small	più piccolo OR minore	il più piccolo OR il minore

*Before nouns, the *e* of these forms is normally dropped (e.g., *il miglior vino; il peggior vino*).

EXAMPLES

Questo vino è più buono. / This wine is better.

OR

Questo vino è migliore.

Quel vino è il più cattivo. / That wine is the worst.

OR

Quel vino è il peggiore.

To express "very" as part of the adjective, just drop the final vowel and add *-issimo*. Don't forget to make this newly-formed adjective agree with the noun!

EXAMPLES

Giovanni è intelligentissimo. / John is very intelligent.
Anche Maria è intelligentissima. / Mary is also very intelligent.

§7.

Pronouns

Pronouns are words used in place of a noun or noun phrase, that is, a noun accompanied by an article or demonstrative (with or without an adjective).

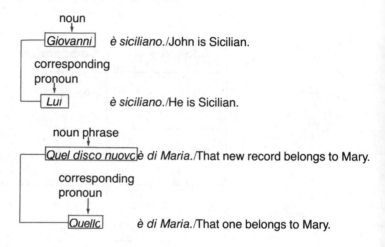

noun
↓
Giovanni è *siciliano.*/John is Sicilian.

corresponding
pronoun
↓
Lui è *siciliano.*/He is Sicilian.

noun phrase
↓
Quel disco nuovo è *di Maria.*/That new record belongs to Mary.

corresponding
pronoun
↓
Quello è *di Maria.*/That one belongs to Mary.

§7.2
DEMONSTRA-
TIVE, POS-
SESSIVE, AND
INTERROGA-
TIVE
PRONOUNS

Demonstrative pronouns replace a noun phrase containing a demonstrative adjective (see §4.2–3).

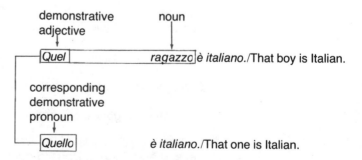

demonstrative   noun
adjective
↓   ↓
Quel   ragazzo è *italiano.*/That boy is Italian.

corresponding
demonstrative
pronoun
↓
Quello è *italiano.*/That one is Italian.

These pronouns correspond to the English "this one," "these," "that one," "those."

● Demonstrative pronouns agree in gender and number with the noun they replace.

Demonstrative Adjectives	Corresponding Demonstrative Pronouns
"this/these"	"this one/these"
	With Masculine Nouns Singular
questo quest'	questo
	Plural
questi	questi
	With Feminine Nouns Singular
questa quest'	questa
	Plural
queste	queste

Demonstrative Adjectives	Corresponding Demonstrative Pronouns
"that/those"	"that one/those"
	With Masculine Nouns Singular
quello quell' quel	quello
	Plural
quegli quei	quelli
	With Feminine Nouns Singular
quella quell'	quella
	Plural
quelle	quelle

EXAMPLES

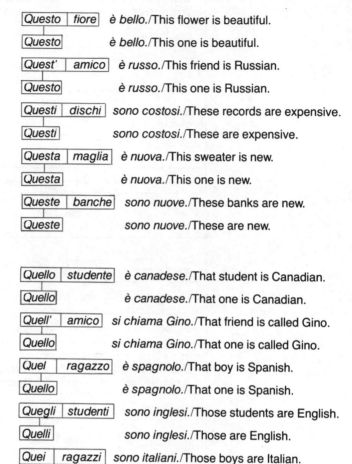

| Questo | fiore | è *bello.*/This flower is beautiful. |

Questo — è *bello.*/This one is beautiful.

Quest' | amico — è *russo.*/This friend is Russian.

Questo — è *russo.*/This one is Russian.

Questi | dischi — sono *costosi.*/These records are expensive.

Questi — sono *costosi.*/These are expensive.

Questa | maglia — è *nuova.*/This sweater is new.

Questa — è *nuova.*/This one is new.

Queste | banche — sono *nuove.*/These banks are new.

Queste — sono *nuove.*/These are new.

Quello | studente — è *canadese.*/That student is Canadian.

Quello — è *canadese.*/That one is Canadian.

Quell' | amico — si *chiama Gino.*/That friend is called Gino.

Quello — si *chiama Gino.*/That one is called Gino.

Quel | ragazzo — è *spagnolo.*/That boy is Spanish.

Quello — è *spagnolo.*/That one is Spanish.

Quegli | studenti — sono *inglesi.*/Those students are English.

Quelli — sono *inglesi.*/Those are English.

Quei | ragazzi — sono *italiani.*/Those boys are Italian.

Quelli — sono *italiani.*/Those are Italian.

Quella | ragazza — è *francese.*/That girl is French.

Quella — è *francese.*/That one is French.

Quelle | studentesse — sono *francesi.*/Those students are French.

Quelle — sono *francesi.*/Those are French.

- Be careful! Some of the forms match exactly; others do not.

  A possessive pronoun replaces a noun phrase containing a possessive adjective (see §6.4–3) and a noun. The Italian possessive pronouns correspond to English "mine," "yours," "his," "hers," "ours," "theirs."

possessive noun
adjective

| Il mio | fidanzato | è bello./My fiancé is handsome.

corresponding
possessive
pronoun

| Il mio | è bello./Mine is handsome.

- In this case there is a perfect match between the adjective and pronoun forms of the possessive. So, just go over the chart in §6.4–3, and it will give you the pronoun forms as well.

EXAMPLES

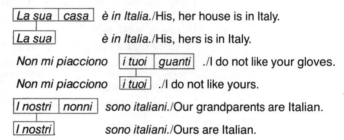

| La sua | casa | è in Italia./His, her house is in Italy.

| La sua | è in Italia./His, hers is in Italy.

Non mi piacciono | i tuoi | guanti | ./I do not like your gloves.

Non mi piacciono | i tuoi | ./I do not like yours.

| I nostri | nonni | sono italiani./Our grandparents are Italian.

| I nostri | sono italiani./Ours are Italian.

- The article is always used with the pronoun forms, even in the case of singular, unmodified, kinship nouns (review §6.4–3).

EXAMPLES

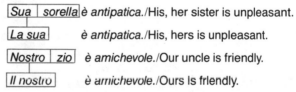

| Sua | sorella | è antipatica./His, her sister is unpleasant.

| La sua | è antipatica./His, hers is unpleasant.

| Nostro | zio | è amichevole./Our uncle is friendly.

| Il nostro | è amichevole./Ours Is frlendly.

- The article can be dropped if the pronoun occurs as a predicate; i.e., if it occurs after the verb *essere* (to be), or some other linking verb (see §6.3).

EXAMPLES
Questo denaro è mio. / This money is mine.
È tua questa borsa? / Is this purse yours?
Quei biglietti sono suoi. / Those tickets are his, hers.

An interrogative pronoun replaces a noun or noun phrase introducing a question. The interrogative adjectives discussed in §6.4–2 of the previous chapter have identical pronoun forms.

EXAMPLES

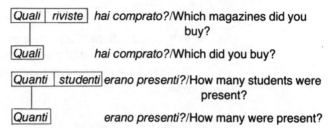

$\boxed{Che \mid libro}$ *leggi?*/What book are you reading?

$\boxed{Che}$ *leggi?*/What are you reading?

> The forms *che, che cosa,* and *cosa* are synonyms for
> "what?" *Che leggi?/Che cosa leggi?/Cosa leggi?*

$\boxed{Quali \mid riviste}$ *hai comprato?*/Which magazines did you
buy?

$\boxed{Quali}$ *hai comprato?*/Which did you buy?

$\boxed{Quanti \mid studenti}$ *erano presenti?*/How many students were
present?

$\boxed{Quanti}$ *erano presenti?*/How many were present?

- Here are a few other useful interrogative pronouns:

chi = who, whom *Chi abita a Roma?*/Who lives in Rome? *Chi conosci qui?*/Whom do you know here?
di chi = whose *Di chi è questo portafoglio?*/Whose wallet is this?
a chi = to whom *A chi hai parlato?*/To whom did you speak?
da chi = from whom *Da chi hai comprato la macchina?*/From whom did you buy the car?

The following words are not, strictly speaking, pronouns.
But since they allow you to ask questions in exactly the
same way, they are listed here for you:

come = how *Come si scrive quella parola?*/How does one write that word?
dove = where *Dove abiti?*/Where do you live?
perché = why *Perché dici così?*/Why do you say that?
quando = when *Quando andrai in Italia?*/When are you going to Italy?

- In writing, it is normal to drop the *e* in *come, dove,* and
  quale before the verb form *è* (is). For both *come* and *dove*
  an apostrophe is used. But this is not the case for *quale!*

> *Com'è?*/How is it?
> *Dov'è?*/Where is it?
>
> BUT
>
> *Qual è?*/Which is it?

§7.3 PERSONAL PRONOUNS

Personal pronouns refer to a person ("I," "you," "we," etc.). They can be classified as a subject, an object, or a reflexive pronoun. Personal pronouns are also classified according to the person speaking (= first person), the person spoken to (= second person), or the person spoken about (= third person). The pronoun can, of course, be in the singular (= referring to one person) or in the plural (= referring to more than one person).

§7.3 – 1 Subject

Subject pronouns are used as the subject of a verb (review the definition of "subject" in §2.1).

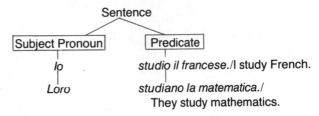

Sentence

Subject Pronoun	Predicate
Io	*studio il francese.*/I study French.
Loro	*studiano la matematica.*/ They study mathematics.

The Italian subject pronouns are:

	Person	Italian Forms	English Equivalents	Examples
S i n g u l a r	1st	*io*	I	*Io non capisco.*/I do not understand.
	2nd	*tu*	you (familiar)	*Tu sei simpatico.*/You are nice
	3rd	*lui*	he	*Lui è americano.*/He is American.
		lei	she	*Lei è americana.*/She is American.
		Lei	you (polite)	*Come si chiama, Lei?*/What is your name?
P l u r a l	1st	*noi*	we	*Noi non lo conosciamo.*/We do not know him.
	2nd	*voi*	you	*Voi arrivate sempre in ritardo.*/You always arrive late.
	3rd	*loro*	they	*Loro vanno in Italia.*/They are going to Italy.
		Loro	you (formal)	*Come si chiamano, Loro?*/What is your name?

- Notice that *io* (I) is not capitalized (unless it is the first word of a sentence).

- Subject pronouns are optional in normal affirmative sentences (see §2.2–1) because it is easy to tell from the verb ending which person is referred to.

  Io non capisco./I do not understand. OR *Non capisco.*

  > tells us
  > that *io* is
  > the subject

  Loro vanno in Italia./They are going to Italy. OR *Vanno in Italia.*

  > tells us
  > that *loro* is
  > the subject

- Sometimes, however, the way a sentence is constructed makes it impossible to avoid using pronouns. This is particularly true when you want to emphasize the subject.

  EXAMPLES
  Devi parlare tu, non io! / You have to speak, not I!
  Non è possibile che l'abbiano fatto loro. / It's not possible that they did it.

- These pronouns must also be used to avoid confusion when more than one person is being referred to.

  EXAMPLES
  Mentre lui guarda la TV, lei ascolta la radio. / While he watches TV, she listens to the radio.
  Lui e io vogliamo che tu dica la verità. / He and I want you to tell the truth.

- They are used after the words *anche* (also, too) and *neanche* (neither, not even) (whose synonyms are *neppure* and *nemmeno*), and *proprio* (really).

  EXAMPLES
  Anche tu devi venire alla festa. / You too must come to the party.
  Non è venuto neanche lui. / He didn't come either.
  Signor Bianchi, è proprio Lei? / Mr. Bianchi, is it really you?

- The subject pronoun "it" usually is not stated in Italian.

  EXAMPLES
  È vero. / It is true.
  Pare che sia corretto. / It appears to be correct.

- However, if you should ever need to express this subject, use *esso* (m.)/*essa* (f.); plural forms: *essi* (m.), *esse* (f.).

È [*una buona scusa*] *, ma neanche* [*essa*] *potrà aiutarti adesso./*
It's a good excuse, but not even it can help you now.

- Notice that "you" has both familiar and polite forms. These are not optional! If you address someone incorrectly, it might be taken as rudeness! So, be careful.

- The familiar forms (and their corresponding verb forms) are used, as the name suggests, with people with whom you are on familiar terms: that is, members of the family, friends, etc. If you call someone by a first name, then you are obviously on familiar terms.

> *Maria, anche tu studi l'italiano?* / Mary, are you studying Italian too?

- The polite forms are used with all other persons.

> *Signora Bianchi, anche Lei studia l'italiano?* / Mrs. Bianchi, are you studying Italian too?

- In writing, the polite forms (*Lei, Loro*) are often capitalized in order to distinguish them from *lei* (she) and *loro* (they), but this is not obligatory.

- In the plural, there is a strong tendency in current Italian to use *voi* as the plural of both *tu* and *Lei. Loro* is restricted to very formal situations (when addressing an audience, when a waiter takes an order, etc.)

"You"		
	Singular	Plural
Familiar	tu	voi
Polite	Lei	Loro (in very formal situations)

- The forms *lui* (he) and *lei* (she) are used in ordinary conversation. However, there are two more formal pronouns that are limited to such things as writing essays: *egli* (he) and *ella* (she).

Normal Conversational Italian

Giovanni è italiano, ma neanche lui capisce i pronomi!/
John is Italian, but he doesn't understand pronouns either!

Formal (Usually Written) Italian

Dante scrisse la Divina Commedia. Egli era fiorentino./
Dante wrote the *Divine Comedy*. He was Florentine.

§7.3 – 2
Object

Object pronouns are used as the object of a verb. As discussed in Chapter 2 (review section §2.2–1), the object can be direct or indirect.

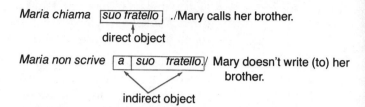

Maria chiama | suo fratello | ./Mary calls her brother.

direct object

Maria non scrive | a | suo | fratello./ Mary doesn't write (to) her brother.

indirect object

The corresponding pronouns are also known as direct and indirect. Italian object pronouns generally come right *before* the verb.

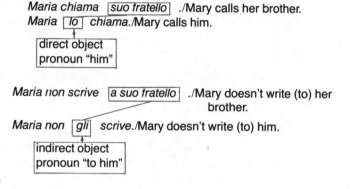

Maria chiama | suo fratello | ./Mary calls her brother.
Maria | lo | chiama./Mary calls him.

direct object
pronoun "him"

Maria non scrive | a suo fratello | ./Mary doesn't write (to) her brother.

Maria non | gli | scrive./Mary doesn't write (to) him.

indirect object
pronoun "to him"

The Italian object pronouns are detailed in the following charts.

- Notice that the first and second person pronouns are identical. Differences occur only in the third person.

- As mentioned in the previous section (see §7.3–1), there are both familiar and polite forms in the singular, but in the plural there is a tendency to use only the second person.

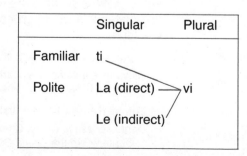

	Singular	Plural
Familiar	ti	
Polite	La (direct)	vi
	Le (indirect)	

Person	Object Pronouns		English Equivalents		Examples
	Direct	**Indirect**			
Singular					
1st	*mi*	*mi*	me	to me	*Maria mi chiama.*/Mary calls me. *Maria mi scrive.*/Mary writes (to) me.
2nd familiar	*ti*	*ti*	you	to you	*Ti chiamo fra mezz'ora.*/I'll call you in a half hour. *Ti scrivo fra un mese.*/I'll write (to) you in a month.
3rd	*lo (m.)*	*gli (m.)*	him	to him	*Maria lo chiama.*/Mary calls him. *Maria gli scrive spesso.*/ Mary writes (to) him often.
	la (f.)	*le (f.)*	her	to her	*Maria la chiama.*/Mary calls her. *Maria le scrive spesso.*/ Mary writes (to) her often.
polite	*La*	*Le*	you	to you	*Signore, La chiamo domani.*/Sir, I'll call you tomorrow. *Signore, Le scrivo fra un mese.*/Sir, I'll write (to) you in a month.
Plural					
1st	*ci*	*ci*	us	to us	*Perché non ci chiami?*/Why don't you call us? *Perché non ci scrivi?*/Why don't you write to us?
2nd	*vi*	*vi*	you	to you	*Domani vi chiamo.*/Tomorrow I'll call you. *Vi scrivo dall'Italia.*/I'll write (to) you from Italy.
3rd	*li (m.)* *le (f.)*	*gli* *gli (f.)*	them them	to them to them	*Li chiamo dopo.*/I'll call them after. *Maria e Claudia? Le chiamo domani, ma non gli scrivo.*/Mary and Claudia? I'll call them tomorrow, but I won't write to them.

- Notice that the plural of the indirect object pronouns *gli* (to him) and *le* (to her) is *gli* (to them). This is very common in current ordinary Italian. However, in more formal situations, some Italians prefer to use *loro* (to them), which goes *after* the verb.

Normal Usage	Very Formal Usage
I ragazzi? Gli parlo domani. / The boys? I'll speak to them tomorrow.	*I signori? Parlo loro domani.* / The gentlemen? I'll speak to them tomorrow.
Le ragazze? Gli parlo domani. / The girls? I'll speak to them tomorrow.	*Le signore? Parlo loro domani.* / The ladies? I'll speak to them tomorrow.

- The English direct object pronoun "it" (plural, "them") is expressed by the third person direct object pronoun. Be careful! Choose the pronoun according to the gender and number of the noun it replaces.

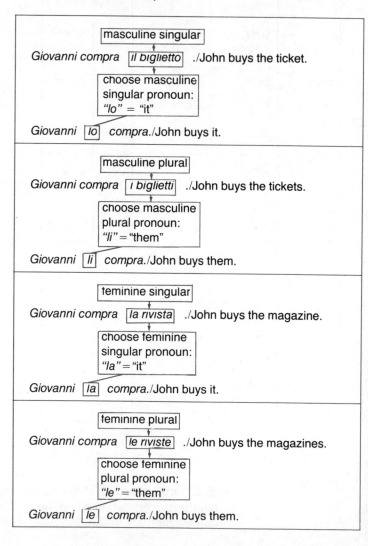

masculine singular

Giovanni compra [il biglietto] *.*/John buys the ticket.

choose masculine singular pronoun: *"lo"* = "it"

Giovanni [lo] *compra.*/John buys it.

masculine plural

Giovanni compra [i biglietti] *.*/John buys the tickets.

choose masculine plural pronoun: *"li"* = "them"

Giovanni [li] *compra.*/John buys them.

feminine singular

Giovanni compra [la rivista] *.*/John buys the magazine.

choose feminine singular pronoun: *"la"* = "it"

Giovanni [la] *compra.*/John buys it.

feminine plural

Giovanni compra [le riviste] *.*/John buys the magazines.

choose feminine plural pronoun: *"le"* = "them"

Giovanni [le] *compra.*/John buys them.

- The past participle of the verb agrees in gender and number with these four pronouns (*lo, la, li, le*) (see Chapter 8 for verb forms using the past participle).

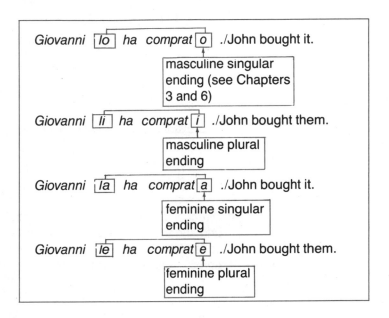

- Note that only the singular forms *lo* and *la* can be elided with the auxiliary forms of *avere: ho, hai, ha, hanno* (see §8.2–2).

  Giovanni lo ha comprato. OR *Giovanni l'ha comprato.*
  Giovanni la ha comprata. OR *Giovanni l'ha comprata.*

- **Agreement with the other direct object pronouns *mi, ti, ci, vi* is optional.**

  Giovanni ci ha chiamato / John called us. (= no agreement)

  OR

  Giovanni ci *ha chiamat* i / John called us. (= agreement)

- Recall that the ending *-i* is used when referring to both male and female persons (review §3.3–1).

- There is *no* agreement with indirect object pronouns.

  Giovanni gli ha scritto. / John wrote (to) him, (to) them.
  Giovanni le ha scritto. / John wrote (to) her.

- But be very careful! The pronoun form *le* has two meanings.

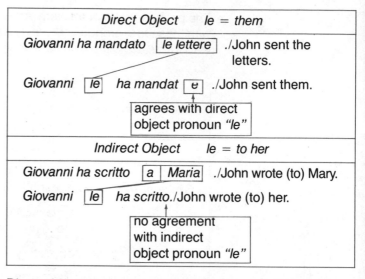

- Direct object pronouns normally follow an infinitive or gerund and are attached to it (see §8.6–1 and §8.6–2). In the case of the infinitive, you must drop the final -e: parlare:→ parlar→parlar*mi*, parlar*ti*, etc.

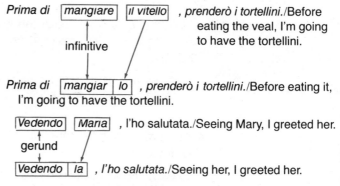

- They are also attached to the form *ecco* (here is, here are, there is, there are) (see §11.3).

  Ecco la ricetta ./Here is the recipe.

  Ecco la ./Here it is.

  Ecco i nostri genitori ./Here are our parents.

  Ecco li ./Here they are.

- With *modal* verbs such as *potere* (to be able to), *dovere* (to have to) and *volere* (to want) (see §8.9), you can either attach the direct object pronoun to the infinitive, or put it before the modal.

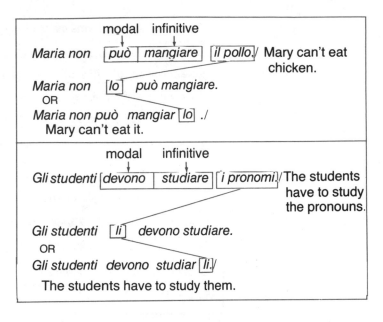

• These pronouns are also attached to the nonpolite forms of the imperative (see §8.3).

Giovanni, paga [*il conto*] *!*/John, pay the bill!

Giovanni, paga[*lo*] *!*/John, pay it!

BUT

Signor Verdi, paghi [*il conto*] *!*/Mr. Verdi, pay the bill!

Signor Verdi, [*lo*] *paghi!*/Mr. Verdi, pay it!

• More will be said about the use of direct object pronouns with imperatives and modal verbs in Chapter 9.

Now comes the complicated task of sequencing indirect and direct objects! Just remember the following, and you won't have too much difficulty:

The indirect object always precedes the direct object *lo, la, li,* or *le.*

Giovanni me lo dà./John gives it to me.

indirect object pronoun   direct object pronoun

> Change the indirect forms *mi, ti, ci, vi* to *me, te, ce,* and *ve,* respectively.

Giovanni mi dà ~~l'indirizzo~~ *./*John gives me the address.
*Giovanni me lo dà./*John gives it to me.

Giovanni ti manda ~~i francobolli~~ *./*John sends you the stamps.
*Giovanni te li manda./*John sends them to you.

Giovanni ci scrive ~~una cartolina~~ */*John writes us a card.
*Giovanni ce la scrive./*John writes it to us.

Giovanni vi scrive ~~una cartolina~~ *./*John writes you a card.
*Giovanni ve la scrive./*John writes it to you.

> Change both the indirect forms *gli* and *le* to *glie,* and combine it with *lo, la, li,* or *le* to form one word: *glielo, glieli, gliela, gliele.*

Lo studente gli porta ~~gli esercizi~~ *./*The student brings the exercises to him, them.
*Lo studente glieli porta./*The student brings them to him, them.

Lo studente le porta ~~le dispense~~ *./*The student brings the course notes to her.
*Lo studente gliele porta./*The student brings them to her.

- When the pronouns are attached to a verb (in the cases discussed above), you always write them as one word.

Prima di mandarti ~~la lettera~~ *, ti telefono./*Before sending you the letter, I'll phone you.
*Prima di mandartela, ti telefono./*Before sending it to you, I'll phone you.

Giovanni, paga ~~il conto~~ ~~al cameriere~~ *!/*John, pay the bill to the waiter!
        lo   gli
*Giovanni, pagaglielo!/*John, pay it to him!

Maria deve comprarmi ~~una borsa~~ *./*Mary has to buy me a purse.
*Maria deve comprarmela./*Mary has to buy it for me.

- And do not forget that when *lo, la, li, le* are put before a past participle, there must be agreement.

*Lo studente gliele ha portate./*The student brought them to her.

- The forms *glielo* and *gliela* can be elided with the auxiliary forms *ho, hai, ha, hanno.*

  Gliel'hanno portato. / They brought it to him, her, them.

  There is a second type of object pronoun that goes after the verb. They are known as *stressed* pronouns.

Before Verb	After Verb	Translation
mi ——————————————— me		me
ti ——————————————— te		you
lo ——	lui	him
gli ——		
la ——	lei	her/you (pol.)
le ——		
ci ——————————————— noi		us
vi ——————————————— voi		you
gli (pl.) ——————————— loro		they

- These allow you to put greater emphasis on the object.

Normal Speech	Emphasis
Maria mi chiama. / Mary calls me.	*Maria chiama me, non te!* / Mary calls me, not you!
Giovanni gli dice la verità. / John tells him the truth.	*Giovanni dice la verità a lui, non a loro!* / John tells him, not them, the truth!

- They also allow you to be precise and clear about the person you are referring to.

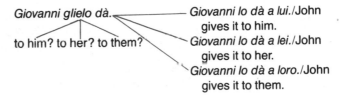

  Giovanni glielo dà. — *Giovanni lo dà a lui.*/John gives it to him.

  to him? to her? to them? — *Giovanni lo dà a lei.*/John gives it to her.

  — *Giovanni lo dà a loro.*/John gives it to them.

- These are the *only* object pronouns you can use after a preposition.

  EXAMPLES

  Maria viene con noi./Mary is coming with us.

  Il professore parla di te./The professor is speaking of you.

  L'ha fatto per me./He did it for me.

§7.3 – 3
Reflexive

Reflexive pronouns, "reflect" the subject of a verb. Like object pronouns, reflexives generally come before the verb.

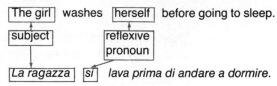

La ragazza si *lava prima di andare a dormire.*

The Italian reflexive pronouns are:

	Person	Italian Forms	English Equivalents	Examples
S **i** **n** **g** **u** **l** **a** **r**	1st	*mi*	myself	*Io mi lavo.*/I wash (myself).
	2nd familiar	*ti*	yourself	*Tu ti diverti.*/You enjoy yourself.
	3rd	*si*	himself, herself, oneself, itself	*Lui si diverte.*/He enjoys himself. *Anche lei si diverte.*/She enjoys herself too.
	3rd polite	*Si*	yourself	*Si diverte, Lei?*/Are you enjoying yourself?
P **l** **u** **r** **a** **l**	1st	*ci*	ourselves	*Anche noi ci divertiamo.*/We too are enjoying ourselves.
	2nd	*vi*	yourselves	*Vi divertite, voi?*/Are you enjoying yourselves?
	3rd	*si*	themselves	*Loro si divertono sempre.*/They always enjoy themselves.
	3rd polite	*Si*	yourselves	*Si divertono, Loro?*/Are you enjoying yourselves?

- Notice that the third person also gives you the polite form of address (which is often capitalized to distinguish it from the other third person forms in writing) (see also §7.3–1).
- These pronouns also express the *reciprocal* forms "to each other," "to themselves," etc.

    Si telefonano ogni sera. / They phone each other every night.
    Noi ci scriviamo ogni mese. / We write each other every month.

- After prepositions (especially *da*), use the forms *me, te, sé, noi, voi.*

    Ci vado da me. / I'm going there by myself.
    Lo farà da sé. / He'll do it by himself.

- Notice that *sé* is written with an accent. However, in the expression *se stesso* ([by] himself), *se stessa* ([by] herself) the accent is omitted.

Ci andrà se stesso. / He'll go by himself.
Maria gli scriverà se stessa. / Mary will write to him herself.

● For more information on these pronouns, see §8.7.

§7.4 RELATIVE PRONOUNS

As discussed in Chapter 2 (review §2.3–1), a relative clause is introduced into a sentence by means of a *relative* pronoun, which serves as a subject or an object in the clause. The relative pronouns in Italian are:

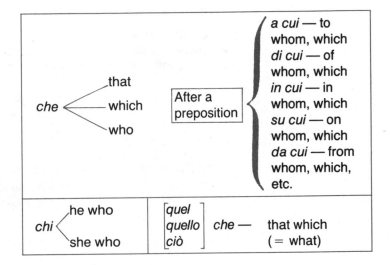

EXAMPLES

che

Quella donna che legge il giornale è mia sorella. / That woman who is reading the newspaper is my sister.

Il vestito che ho comprato ieri è molto bello. / The dress I bought yesterday is very beautiful

Mi piace la poesia che stai leggendo. / I like the poem (that) you are reading.

cui

Il ragazzo a cui ho dato il regalo è mio cugino./The boy to whom I gave the gift is my cousin.

Non trovo il cassetto in cui ho messo il mio anello./I can't find the drawer in which I put my ring.

Ecco la rivista di cui ho parlato./Here is the magazine of which I spoke.

chi

Chi va in Italia si divertirà. / He, she who goes to Italy will enjoy himself, herself.
C'è chi dorme e c'è chi lavora! / Some sleep, some work! (*lit.*, There is he who sleeps and there is he who works!)

quel/quello/ciò che

Quello che dici è vero. / What (that which) you are saying is true.
Non sai quel che dici. / You don't know what you are saying.

- Both *che* and *cui* can be replaced by *il quale*, if there is an antecedent. It changes in form according to the noun it refers to and is always preceded by the definite article.

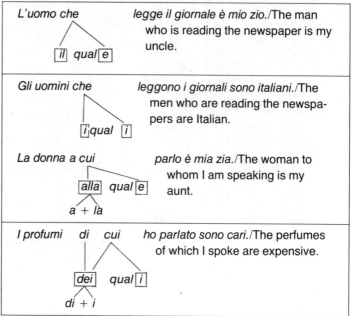

L'uomo che [il] qual[e] *legge il giornale è mio zio.*/The man who is reading the newspaper is my uncle.

Gli uomini che [i] qual [i] *leggono i giornali sono italiani.*/The men who are reading the newspapers are Italian.

La donna a cui [alla] qual[e] (a + la) *parlo è mia zia.*/The woman to whom I am speaking is my aunt.

I profumi   di   cui [dei] qual[i] (di + i) *ho parlato sono cari.*/The perfumes of which I spoke are expensive.

- When there is no antecedent, only *che* is used.
- *Il quale, la quale,* etc., are used when you want to be clear about which noun is being referred to.
- To express "whose," use *il cui,* changing the article according to the gender and number of the noun modified.

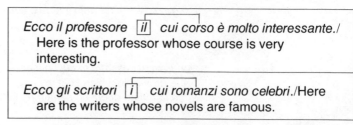

Ecco il professore [il] *cui corso è molto interessante.*/ Here is the professor whose course is very interesting.

Ecco gli scrittori [i] *cui romanzi sono celebri.*/Here are the writers whose novels are famous.

Ecco la ragazza | la | *cui intelligenza è straordinaria./*
Here is the girl whose intelligence is extraordinary.

Ecco la ragazza | le | *cui amiche sono italiane./*Here
is the girl whose friends are Italian.

§7.5 OTHER PRONOUNS

The indefinite adjectives discussed in Chapter 6 have corresponding indefinite pronouns. The pronouns have only one form (review the chart in §6.4–4).

EXAMPLES

Lui mangia assai. He eats quite a lot.
Tuo fratello dorme molto, no? / Your brother sleeps a lot, doesn't he?
Ieri ho mangiato troppo. / Yesterday I ate too much.

- When referring to people in general, use the plural forms *molti, alcuni, tanti, pochi, parecchi, tutti,* etc.

EXAMPLES

Molti vanno in Italia quest'anno. / Many are going to Italy this year.
Alcuni dormono alla mattina, ma parecchi lavorano già. / Some sleep in the morning, but quite a few are working already.
Tutti sanno quello. / Everyone knows that.

- Use the corresponding feminine forms (*molte, alcune,* etc.) when referring only to females.

EXAMPLES

Di quelle ragazze, molte sono italiane. / Of those girls, many are Italian.
Di tutte quelle donne, alcune sono americane. / Of all those women, some are American.

- Notice the expression *alcuni . . . altri* (some . . . others).

Alcuni andranno in Italia; altri, invece, andranno in Francia. / Some will go to Italy; others, instead, will go to France.

The pronoun *ne* has four main functions. It is used to replace:

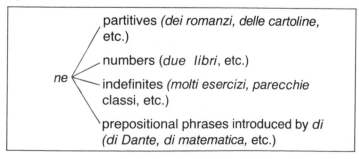

ne —
- partitives (*dei romanzi, delle cartoline,* etc.)
- numbers (*due libri,* etc.)
- indefinites (*molti esercizi, parecchie classi,* etc.)
- prepositional phrases introduced by *di* (*di Dante, di matematica,* etc.)

Like most object pronouns, it is usually placed before the verb (except in those cases discussed in §7.3–2).

EXAMPLES

Partitive: *ne* = "some"

Domani scriverò delle cartoline ./Tomorrow I'm going to write some postcards.

Domani ne *scriverò.*/Tomorrow I'm going to write some.

Anch'io devo comprare della carne ./I too have to buy some meat.

Anch'io ne *devo comprare.*/I too have to buy some.

Numbers: *ne* = "of them" (retain the number)

Domani comprerò tre matite ./Tomorrow I will buy three pencils.

Domani ne *comprerò* tre ./Tomorrow I will buy three (of them).

Voglio comprare quattro dischi ./I want to buy four records.

Ne *voglio comprare* quattro ./I want to buy four (of them).

Indefinites: *ne* = "of them" (retain the indefinite)

Domani vedrò molte amiche ./Tomorrow I'm going to see many (female) friends.

Domani ne *vedrò* molte ./Tomorrow I'm going to see many of them.

Devo comprare parecchi regali ./I have to buy quite a few presents.

Ne *devo comprare* parecchi ./I have to buy quite a few of them.

Phrases introduced by *di*: *ne* = "of him, her, it, them"/"about him, her," etc.

Il professore parlerà di matematica ./The professor will speak about mathematics.

Il professore ne *parlerà.*/The professor will speak about it.

Lei parlerà del suo amico ./She will speak about her friend.

Lei ne *parlerà.*/She will speak about him.

- When replacing partitives, numbers, and definites, there is agreement between *ne* and the past participle. This is not the case when *ne* replaces a phrase introduced by *di*.

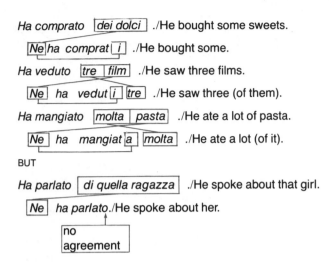

Ha comprato dei dolci ./He bought some sweets.

Ne ha comprat i ./He bought some.

Ha veduto tre film ./He saw three films.

Ne ha vedut i tre ./He saw three (of them).

Ha mangiato molta pasta ./He ate a lot of pasta.

Ne ha mangiat a molta ./He ate a lot (of it).

BUT

Ha parlato di quella ragazza ./He spoke about that girl.

Ne ha parlato./He spoke about her.

no agreement

The pronoun *ci* (identical to the object and reflexive *ci* discussed above) can also mean "there." As always, it goes before the verb (except in the cases mentioned in §7.3–2).

ci = "there"

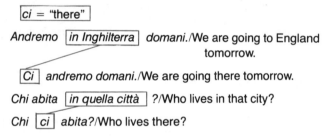

Andremo in Inghilterra *domani.*/We are going to England tomorrow.

Ci *andremo domani.*/We are going there tomorrow.

Chi abita in quella città ?/Who lives in that city?

Chi ci *abita?*/Who lives there?

• However, to express "from there," you have to use *ne* (again!).

Tu vai in Italia , *e io vengo* dall'Italia./You are going to Italy, and I'm coming from Italy.

Tu ci *vai, e io* ne *vengo.*/You are going there, and I'm coming from there.

In these cases, there is no agreement between *ci* and *ne* and the past participle.

Both *ci* and *ne* can occur in sequence with object pronouns.

Ci is changed to *ce* when it precedes other pronouns.

Io metto il portafoglio nel cassetto ./I put my wallet in the drawer.

Io ce lo *metto.*/I put it there.

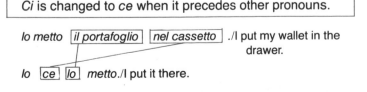

> *Ne* is placed after the indirect object pronouns in the normal fashion.

Giovanni mi dà ⟦*delle rose*⟧ *.*/John gives me some roses.

Giovanni me ne dà./John gives some to me.

Il medico gli dà ⟦*delle pillole*⟧ *.*/The doctor gives him some pills.

Il medico gliene dà./The doctor gives some to him.

And now for the last pronoun to be discussed! The impersonal *si* (one, in general) has the following peculiar characteristics:

> Unlike its synonym *uno*, with *si* the verb agrees with what appears to be the predicate!

Uno compra quel libro solo in Italia./One buys that book only in Italy.

Si compra quel libro solo in Italia.

Uno compra quei libri solo in Italia./One buys those books only in Italy.

Si comprano quei libri solo in Italia.

> All compound tenses using *si* (see §8.2–2), are conjugated with *essere* (to be), with the past participle agreeing, apparently, with the predicate!

Uno ha veduto quei film solo in Italia./One has seen those films only in Italy.

Si sono vedut ⟦*i*⟧ *quei film solo in Italia.*

> When followed by a predicate adjective (see §6.3), the adjective is always in the plural (usually in -*i*!).

Uno è contento in Italia./One is happy in Italy.

Si è content ⟦*i*⟧ *in Italia.*

> Direct object pronouns are placed before it!

Uno deve dire ⟦*la verità*⟧ *.*/One has to tell the truth.

Uno ⟦*la*⟧ *deve dire.*/One has to tell it.

⟦*La*⟧ *si deve dire.*

In front of the reflexive *si* (see §7.3–3)/"oneself", *si* changes
to *ci*!

Uno si diverte in Italia./One enjoys oneself in Italy.
    |
Si
    |
Ci si diverte in Italia.

§8.

Verbs

§8.1
WHAT ARE
VERBS?

Verbs are words that indicate the action performed by the subject. For this reason, the verb agrees with the subject's *person* (first, second, third — see §7.3) and *number* (singular or plural).

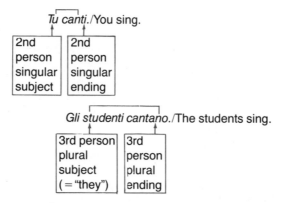

Tu canti./You sing.

| 2nd person singular subject | 2nd person singular ending |

Gli studenti cantano./The students sing.

| 3rd person plural subject (= "they") | 3rd person plural ending |

- For the kinds of objects that verbs can take, go over §2.2–1.

- In Italian a verb is listed in a dictionary in its infinitive form (see also §8.6–1). Italian verbs are divided into three conjugations according to their infinitive endings.

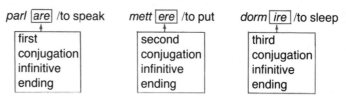

| *parl* are /to speak | *mett* ere /to put | *dorm* ire /to sleep |
| first conjugation infinitive ending | second conjugation infinitive ending | third conjugation infinitive ending |

- These infinitive endings allow you to determine which person and number endings a verb must take when you conjugate it (that is, when you attach the endings to the verb according to some pattern).

- A verb tense indicates the time the action occurred: *now* (present tense), *before* (past tense), or *after* (future tense).

  La mangio adesso. / I'm eating it now. (present tense)
  L'ho mangiata ieri. / I ate it yesterday. (past tense)
  La mangerò domani. / I will eat it tomorrow. (future tense)

- Not only do verbs allow you to express a time relationship but they also allow you to convey your manner of thinking, point of view, etc. This aspect of a verb is known as its *mood*.

Maria scrive la lettera. (indicative mood—states something)
Maria, scrivi la lettera! / Mary, write the letter! (imperative mood—allows you to make commands)

È probabile che Maria scriva la lettera./ It's probable that Mary is writing the letter (subjunctive mood—allows you to express probability, doubt, etc.)

We will first study the tenses of the different moods of *regular* verbs. A regular verb is one whose conjugations follow a general pattern. Verbs that do not are known as *irregular.* You will find some common irregular verbs in the "Verb Charts" section at the end of this book.

§8.2
THE INDICA-TIVE TENSES

The *indicative* mood allows you to express or indicate facts. It is used for ordinary statements and questions, and is the most commonly used mood in everyday conversation.

§8.2 – 1
Present

The present tense is formed as follows:

• Drop the infinitive ending of the verb and add the following endings to the stem according to the conjugation.

	Person	Endings		
		1st Conjugation = are	2nd Conjugation = ere	3rd Conjugation = ire
Singular	1st	-o	-o	-o
	2nd	-i	-i	-i
	3rd	-a	-e	-e
Plural	1st	-iamo	-iamo	-iamo
	2nd	-ate	-ete	-ite
	3rd	-ano	-ono	-ono

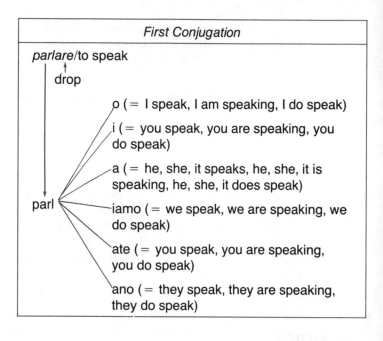

First Conjugation

parlare/to speak

↑ drop

parl —
- o (= I speak, I am speaking, I do speak)
- i (= you speak, you are speaking, you do speak)
- a (= he, she, it speaks, he, she, it is speaking, he, she, it does speak)
- iamo (= we speak, we are speaking, we do speak)
- ate (= you speak, you are speaking, you do speak)
- ano (= they speak, they are speaking, they do speak)

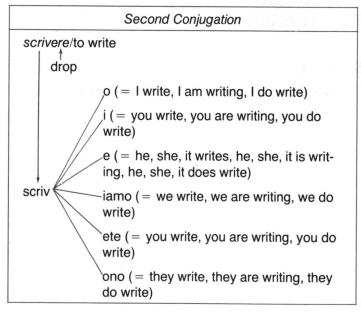

Second Conjugation

scrivere/to write

↑ drop

scriv —
- o (= I write, I am writing, I do write)
- i (= you write, you are writing, you do write)
- e (= he, she, it writes, he, she, it is writing, he, she, it does write)
- iamo (= we write, we are writing, we do write)
- ete (= you write, you are writing, you do write)
- ono (= they write, they are writing, they do write)

EXAMPLES

Lui parla molto bene. / He speaks very well.
Quando scrivi quella lettera? / When are you writing that letter?
Non apriamo mai le finestre d'inverno. / We never open the windows in the winter.
È vero; lei scrive molto bene. / It's very true; she does write very well.

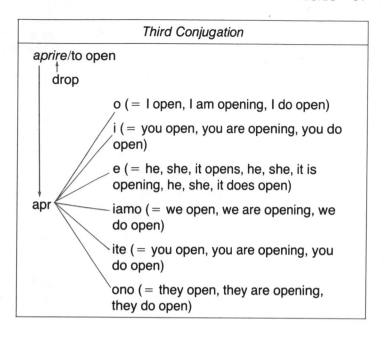

Third Conjugation

aprire/to open

drop

apr
- o (= I open, I am opening, I do open)
- i (= you open, you are opening, you do open)
- e (= he, she, it opens, he, she, it is opening, he, she, it does open)
- iamo (= we open, we are opening, we do open)
- ite (= you open, you are opening, you do open)
- ono (= they open, they are opening, they do open)

- There is a second type of third conjugation verb that has an additional -isc- in front of the endings -o, -i, -e, and -ono.

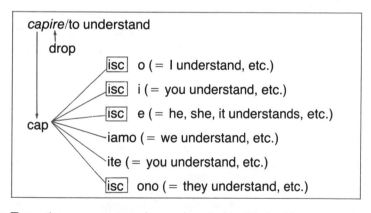

capire/to understand

drop

cap
- isc o (= I understand, etc.)
- isc i (= you understand, etc.)
- isc e (= he, she, it understands, etc.)
- iamo (= we understand, etc.)
- ite (= you understand, etc.)
- isc ono (= they understand, etc.)

- Two other common verbs conjugated in this fashion are finire (to finish) and preferire (to prefer).

EXAMPLES

Gli studenti non capiscono la lezione. / The students do not understand the lesson.
Finisco di lavorare alle sei. / I finish working at six.
Quale preferisce, Lei? / Which one do you (pol.) prefer?

- You will have to learn whether a given third conjugation verb follows this pattern or the other one (aprire). A good dictionary will provide this kind of information.

- Be careful when you pronounce the third person plural forms! The accent is *not* placed on the ending.

  parlano/they speak

  ↑
  stress

  scrivono/they write

  ↑
  stress

- Recall from the previous chapter (see §7.3–1) that subject pronouns are optional with the indicative tenses. The reason is obvious: the endings make it clear which person is being referred to.

- The third person forms are used, of course, with subjects that are not pronouns.

  La ragazza *studi* a ./The girl studies.

  Quegli studenti non studi ano ./Those students do not study.

- Remember as well (§7.3–1) that for the singular polite "you," the third person singular form is used.

  Cosa preferisci, tu? / What do you (*fam.*) prefer?
  Cosa preferisce, Lei? / What do you (*pol.*) prefer?

- And do not forget that the subject pronoun "it" (plural "they") is not normally expressed (§7.3–1).

  Apre a mezzogiorno. / It opens at noon.

- In the first conjugation only, if a verb ends in hard *c* or hard *g* before the ending *-are*, you retain the hard sound by adding an *h* before the endings *-i* and *-iamo*.

  cercare / to search for

  cerco / I search
  cerchi / you search
  cerca / he, she, it searches
  cerchiamo / we search
  cercate / you search
  cercano / they search

  pagare / to pay (for)

  pago / I pay
  paghi / you pay
  paga / he, she, it pays
  paghiamo / we pay
  pagate / you pay
  pagano / they pay

- Also in the first conjugation, if a verb ends in soft *c* or soft *g*, written as *-ciare* and *-giare*, then you do not keep the *i* before *-i* or *-iamo*.

  cominciare / to start, begin

  comincio / I start
  cominci / you start
  comincia / he, she, it starts
  cominciamo / we start
  cominciate / you start
  cominciano / they start

  mangiare / to eat

  mangio / I eat
  mangi / you eat
  mangia / he, she, it eats
  mangiam / we eat
  mangiate / you eat
  mangiano / they eat

- This is not applicable to the second and third conjugations.

● Note that the Italian present indicative is equivalent to three English verb tenses.

I speak

parlo ⟵ _I am speaking_

I do speak

● In addition, it can be used with the preposition _da_ (which, in this case, means both "since" and "for") to express the present perfect progressive tense in English.

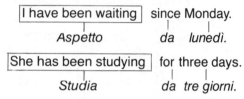

| I have been waiting | since Monday. |

Aspetto   _da   lunedì._

| She has been studying | for three days. |

Studia   _da tre giorni._

● Finally, you can use this versatile tense to express a future action that is not too far off in the future.

> _Domani andiamo al teatro._ / Tomorrow we are going to the theater.
> _Domani parlo al professore._ / Tomorrow I will speak to the professor.

§8.2 – 2
Present
Perfect

The present perfect tense expresses simple past actions in the indicative mood (see also §8.2–3). It is a compound tense, that is, it is formed by the appropriate form of the auxiliary verb plus the past participle of the verb, in that order.

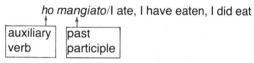

ho mangiato/I ate, I have eaten, I did eat

| auxiliary | past |
| verb | participle |

● To form the past participle of regular verbs in Italian, drop the infinitive ending and add the following endings:

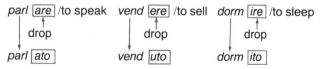

parl |are| /to speak   _vend_ |ere| /to sell   _dorm_ |ire| /to sleep

drop   drop   drop

parl |ato| _vend_ |uto| _dorm_ |ito|

● In Italian there are two auxiliary verbs: _avere_ (to have) and _essere_ (to be). In the present perfect, these verbs are conjugated, logically enough, in the present indicative. Both are irregular, and you will find their conjugations in the "Verb Charts" section. The three verbs listed above are conjugated with _avere_.

ho	*parlato* (= I spoke, I have spoken, I did speak) *venduto* (= I sold, etc.) *dormito* (= I slept, etc.)
hai	*parlato* (= you spoke, etc.) *venduto* (= you sold, etc.) *dormito* (= you slept, etc.)
ha	*parlato* (= he, she, it spoke, etc.) *venduto* (= he, she, it sold, etc.) *dormito* (= he, she, it slept, etc.)
abbiamo	*parlato* (= we spoke, etc.) *venduto* (= we sold, etc.) *dormito* (= we slept, etc.)
avete	*parlato* (= you spoke, etc.) *venduto* (= you sold, etc.) *dormito* (= you slept, etc.)
hanno	*parlato* (= they spoke, etc.) *venduto* (= they sold, etc.) *dormito* (= they slept, etc.)

EXAMPLES

Maria ha venduto la sua macchina. / Mary sold her car.
Ieri ho parlato al signor Verdi. / Yesterday, I spoke to Mr. Verdi.
Loro hanno dormìto troppo ieri. / They slept too much yesterday.
Ho già mangiato. / I have already eaten.

- The verbs *arrivare* (to arrive), *cadere* (to fall), and *partire* (to leave, depart) are conjugated with *essere*. In this case, the final vowel of the past participle agrees with the subject in the same way that an adjective does (see §6.2).

Singular		
(io) sono	*arrivato* (-a) *caduto* (-a) *partito* (-a)	(= I arrived) (= I fell) (= I left)
(tu) sei	*arrivato* (-a) *caduto* (-a) *partito* (-a)	(= you arrived) (= you fell) (= you left)
(lui) è	*arrivato* *caduto* *partito*	(= he arrived) (= he fell) (= he left)

Singular		
(lei) è	*arrivata*	(= she arrived)
	caduta	(= she fell)
	partita	(= she left)

- Remember that *Lei* is the polite form of address. In this case, choose the ending according to the sex of the person you are addressing.

    Signor Verdi, è caduto, Lei? / Mr. Verdi, did you fall?
    Signora Verdi, è caduta, Lei? / Mrs. Verdi, did you fall?

- In the plural, do not forget that the masculine ending *-i* refers to people of both genders (review §6.2).

Plural			
(noi) siamo	*arrivati*	*(-e)*	(= we arrived)
	caduti	*(-e)*	(= we fell)
	partiti	*(-e)*	(= we left)
(voi) siete	*arrivati*	*(-e)*	(= you arrived)
	caduti	*(-e)*	(= you fell)
	partiti	*(-e)*	(= you left)
(loro) sono	*arrivati*	*(-e)*	(= they arrived)
	caduti	*(-e)*	(= they fell)
	partiti	*(-e)*	(= they left)

- Do not forget all the things you know about the use of subject pronouns with the indicative (see §7.3–1).

- When do you use *avere* or *essere*? The answer to this question is quite complicated. The best learning strategy is to assume that most verbs are conjugated with *avere* (which is true!), and then memorize those few verbs conjugated with *essere*. Here are some of them. Notice that these verbs are all intransitive.

andare/to go	*nascere*/to be born
arrivare/to arrive	*partire*/to leave, depart
cadere/to fall	*stare*/to stay, remain
entrare/to enter	*sembrare*/to seem
essere/to be	*tornare*/to return
diventare/to become	*uscire*/to go out
morire/to die	*venire*/to come

- There are a few verbs that are never conjugated in the normal fashion with a subject pronoun. These *impersonal* verbs occur only in the third person form, and are conjugated with *essere*.

    Lo spettacolo è durato tre ore. / The show lasted three hours.

- Remember! To be sure about which auxiliary to use, look up the main verb in a good dictionary.

- Notice that this tense is also equivalent to three English tenses.

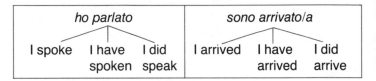

ho parlato			*sono arrivato/a*		
I spoke	I have spoken	I did speak	I arrived	I have arrived	I did arrive

- Recall that the past participle must agree with the direct object pronouns *lo, la, li, le* (§7.3–2) and the pronoun *ne* (§7.5).

  Le ho mangiate./I ate them.

  Ne ho mangiati tre./I ate three of them.

- Only verbs conjugated with *avere* can have *direct object* pronouns.

§8.2 – 3 Imperfect

As you know, the present perfect allows you to express a finished past action, that is, an action you visualize as having started and ended.

> *Ieri ho dormito due ore.*/Yesterday I slept (for) two hours.

If, however, you wish to indicate that an action continued for an indefinite period of time, then the imperfect tense is called for.

> *Ieri, mentre io dormivo, tu guardavi la TV.*/Yesterday, while I was sleeping, you watched TV.

The imperfect is used to indicate that an action was habitual or repeated in the past.

> *Quando ero giovane, suonavo il pianoforte.*/When I was young, I used to play the piano.

It is also used to describe the physical characteristics of people and things as they used to be in the past.

> *Da giovane, Maria aveva i capelli biondi.*/As a youth, Mary had (= used to have) blonde hair.

- To form the imperfect, drop the infinitive ending and add the following endings (see §8.2–1):

	Person	Endings		
		1st Conj. = are	2nd Conj. = ere	3rd Conj. = ire
S i n g u l a r	1st	-avo	-evo	-ivo
	2nd	-avi	-evi	-ivi
	3rd	-ava	-eva	-iva
P l u r a l	1st	-avamo	-evamo	-ivamo
	2nd	-avate	-evate	-ivate
	3rd	-avano	-evano	-ivano

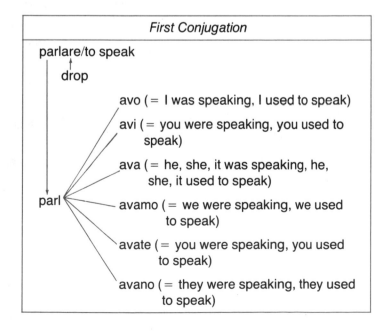

First Conjugation

parlare/to speak
    ↑
   drop
 	
parl avo (= I was speaking, I used to speak)
    avi (= you were speaking, you used to speak)
    ava (= he, she, it was speaking, he, she, it used to speak)
    avamo (= we were speaking, we used to speak)
    avate (= you were speaking, you used to speak)
    avano (= they were speaking, they used to speak)

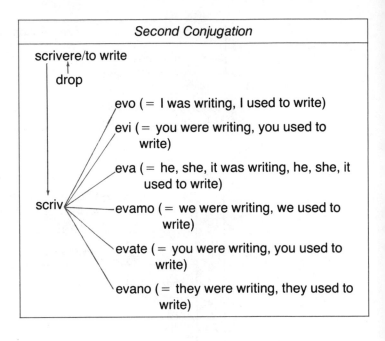

Second Conjugation

scrivere/to write

↑ drop

scriv ＜
- evo (= I was writing, I used to write)
- evi (= you were writing, you used to write)
- eva (= he, she, it was writing, he, she, it used to write)
- evamo (= we were writing, we used to write)
- evate (= you were writing, you used to write)
- evano (= they were writing, they used to write)

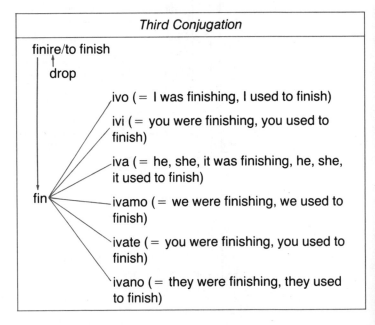

Third Conjugation

finire/to finish

↑ drop

fin ＜
- ivo (= I was finishing, I used to finish)
- ivi (= you were finishing, you used to finish)
- iva (= he, she, it was finishing, he, she, it used to finish)
- ivamo (= we were finishing, we used to finish)
- ivate (= you were finishing, you used to finish)
- ivano (= they were finishing, they used to finish)

EXAMPLES

Mentre tu studiavi, tuo fratello suonava il violino. / While you were studying, your brother was playing the violin.

L'anno scorso mio cugino scriveva ogni mese. / Last year my
                                    cousin wrote
                                    (used to write)
                                    every month.
Quando andava a scuola, Maria studiava molto. / When she was
                                    going to
                                    school, Mary
                                    studied
                                    (used to
                                    study) a lot.

- Note that the third person plural forms are *not* stressed on the last syllable.

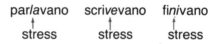

par*la*vano   scri*ve*vano   fi*ni*vano
   ↑   ↑   ↑
 stress   stress   stress

- The Italian imperfect is equivalent to two English tenses:

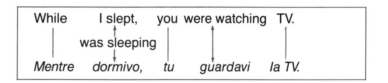

parlavo ⟨ I was speaking
          ⟨ I used to speak

- Sometimes English uses a perfect form that is normally covered by the Italian present perfect (§8.2–1). In all cases, this is merely another way of expressing an imperfect action.

While	I slept,	you	were watching	TV.
	was sleeping			
Mentre	*dormivo,*	*tu*	*guardavi*	*la TV.*

- But in the following example, no such equivalence exists.

Yesterday	I slept	for only two hours.
Ieri	*ho dormito*	*solo due ore.*

- You must therefore always look for clues among the other words in a sentence to determine whether the imperfect should be used. Words such as *mentre* (while) and *sempre* (always) often indicate that a past action is imperfect in the dependent clause.

§8.2 – 4
Past Absolute

As we shall soon see, the uses of the past absolute are similar, in many ways, to the present perfect (§8.2–2). It is formed by dropping the infinitive ending and then adding the following endings to the stem:

	Person	Endings		
		1st Conjugation = are	**2nd Conjugation = ere**	**3rd Conjugation = ire**
S i n g u l a r	1st	-ai	-ei (-etti)	-ii
	2nd	-asti	-esti	-isti
	3rd	-ò	-è (-ette)	-ì
P l u r a l	1st	-ammo	-emmo	-immo
	2nd	-aste	-este	-iste
	3rd	-arono	-erono (-ettero)	-irono

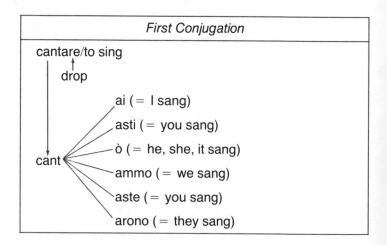

First Conjugation

cantare/to sing
↑
drop

cant
- ai (= I sang)
- asti (= you sang)
- ò (= he, she, it sang)
- ammo (= we sang)
- aste (= you sang)
- arono (= they sang)

EXAMPLES

I miei genitori tornarono in Italia nel 1976. / My parents returned to Italy in 1976.

Marco Polo portò tante belle cose indietro dalla Cina. / Marco Polo brought back many beautiful things from China.

Dopo che vendè (vendette) la macchina, Gino comprò una motocicletta. / After he sold the car, Gino bought a motorcycle.

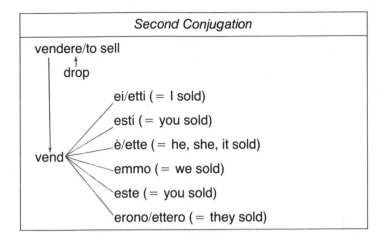

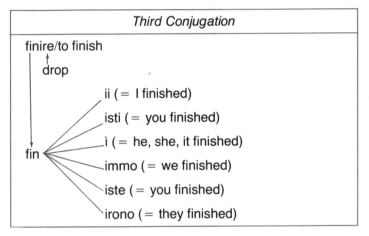

- Recall that the present perfect is equivalent to three English tenses (§8.2—2). One of these tenses is also covered by the past absolute.

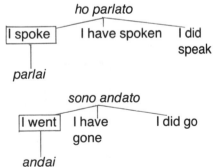

- However, the past absolute cannot be used with temporal adverbs such as *già* (already), *poco fa* (a little while ago), etc., which limit the action to the immediate past (occurring within less than twenty-four hours).

Only Present Perfect Used:

Maria è arrivata poco tempo fa. / Mary arrived a little while ago.
Ho già telefonato al signor Rossi. / I have already phoned Mr. Rossi.

- Outside this time restriction, the past absolute can be used as an alternative to the present perfect to cover the English perfect tense exemplified above (I spoke, I went, etc.).

Present Perfect		Past Absolute
Maria è arrivata in Italia nel 1980. / Mary arrived in Italy in 1980.	OR	*Maria arrivò in Italia nel 1980.*
Ieri ho telefonato al signor Rossi. / Yesterday I phoned Mr. Rossi.	OR	*Ieri telefonai al signor Rossi.*

- In Italy you will find that certain regions use one or the other tense in ordinary conversational situations. But the past absolute is preferred as a "literary" tense, particularly for the narration of historical events.

Colombo scoprì l'America nel 1492. / Columbus discovered America in 1492.

- Whatever tense you decide to use (following the above restrictions), you must use either tense consistently when several clauses are involved.

Quando sono arrivati, hanno telefonato a Maria. / When they arrived, they phoned Mary.

Quando arrivarano, telefonarono a Maria.

- If you have forgotten about clauses, review §2.3–1.

§8.2 – 5 Pluperfect

The pluperfect is a compound tense. As such, it has all the characteristics associated with this kind of verb form. (Review §8.2–2 of this chapter if you have forgotten about compound tenses.)

- The pluperfect is formed with the auxiliary in the imperfect tense (§8.2–3).

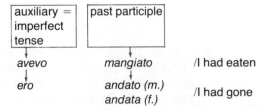

auxiliary = imperfect tense	past participle	
avevo	*mangiato*	/ I had eaten
ero	*andato (m.)* *andata (f.)*	/ I had gone

- Here are these two verbs fully conjugated:

avevo mangiato / **I had eaten**	*ero andato(-a)* / **I had gone**
avevi mangiato / **you had eaten**	*eri andato(-a)* / **you had gone**
aveva mangiato / **he, she, it had eaten**	*era andato(-a)* / **he, she, it had gone**
avevamo mangiato / **we had eaten**	*eravamo andati(-e)* / **we had gone**
avevate mangiato / **you had eaten**	*eravate andati(-e)* / **you had gone**
avevano mangiato / **they had eaten**	*erano andati(-e)* / **they had gone**

- If you have forgotten the rule of thumb on using one auxiliary verb or the other, go over §8.2–2.

- The pluperfect tense (literally, "more than perfect" or "more than past") allows you to express an action that occurred *before* a simple past action (as expressed by the present perfect, the imperfect, or the past absolute).

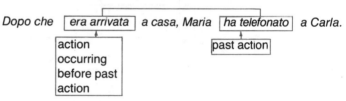

After she had arrived home, Mary phoned Carla.

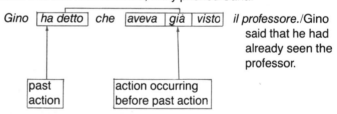

- As you can see, this tense is rendered by the corresponding English pluperfect ("had" + past participle). But be careful! Sometimes this tense is only implied in English.

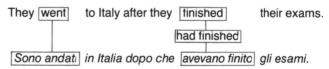

- Therefore, you will generally use this tense in dependent clauses, especially those introduced by a temporal conjunction (review §2.3–2).

- There exists another pluperfect tense that is limited to very formal literary usage. But it is used so seldom that you will probably never need it.

§8.2 – 6
Simple Future

The simple future, as its name implies, allows you to express an action that will occur in the future. It is formed in the following manner:

- Drop the final *-e* of the infinitives of all three conjugations. For verbs of the first conjugation (*-are*), change the *a* of the infinitive to *e*.

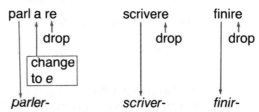

parl a re   scrivere   finire

↑ drop   ↑ drop   ↑ drop

| change to e |

parler-   *scriver-*   *finir-*

Then add the following endings to all three conjugations.

	Person	Endings for all Conjugations
S i n g u l a r	1st	-ò
	2nd	-ai
	3rd	-à
P l u r a l	1st	-emo
	2nd	-ete
	3rd	-anno

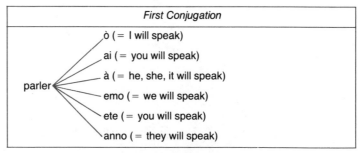

First Conjugation
ò (= I will speak)
ai (= you will speak)
à (= he, she, it will speak)
parler emo (= we will speak)
ete (= you will speak)
anno (= they will speak)

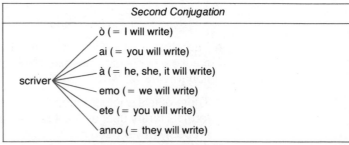

Second Conjugation
ò (= I will write)
ai (= you will write)
à (= he, she, it will write)
scriver emo (= we will write)
ete (= you will write)
anno (= they will write)

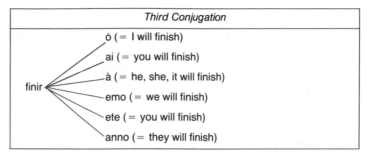

Third Conjugation
finir ← ò (= I will finish)
ai (= you will finish)
à (= he, she, it will finish)
emo (= we will finish)
ete (= you will finish)
anno (= they will finish)

- Recall that the hard *c* and hard *g* sounds are retained in first conjugation verbs by adding an *h* (see §8.2–1). This is the case for the future tense too. In writing, add the *h*.

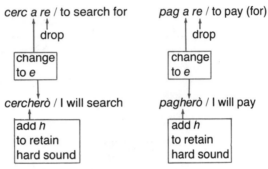

cerc a re / to search for
↑↑
drop

change
to *e*

cercherò / I will search
↑
add *h*
to retain
hard sound

pag a re / to pay (for)
↑↑
drop

change
to *e*

pagherò / I will pay
↑
add *h*
to retain
hard sound

- Similarly, remember that to write the corresponding soft sounds, you omit the *i* of the infinitive (see §8.2–1).

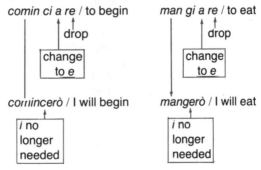

comin ci a re / to begin
↑↑
drop

change
to *e*

comincerò / I will begin
↑
i no
longer
needed

man gi a re / to eat
↑↑
drop

change
to *e*

mangerò / I will eat
↑
i no
longer
needed

- The future tense is normally rendered by the English future ("I will go," etc.). It can also be translated by using the expression "going to."

> *Scriverò.* / I will write OR I'm going to write.
> *Partiranno domani.* / They will leave tomorrow OR They are going to leave tomorrow.

- This tense is also used to express probability.

> *Quanto costa il tuo orologio?* / How much does your watch cost?
> *Costerà centomila lire.* / It must cost a hundred thousand lira.

- It can be used as well in temporal clauses introduced by *se* (if), *quando* (when), and *appena* (as soon as) (see §2.3–2) in order to agree with a future tense in the main clause.

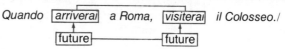

Quando arriverai *a Roma,* visiterai *il Colosseo./*

When you arrive in Rome, you will visit the Colosseum.

§8.2 – 7
Future Perfect

Like the present perfect (see §8.2–2) and the pluperfect (see §8.2–5), the future perfect is a compound tense.

- In this case, the auxiliary is in the future tense.

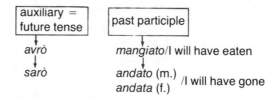

auxiliary = future tense	past participle
avrò	mangiato/I will have eaten
sarò	andato (m.) andata (f.) /I will have gone

- Here are these two verbs fully conjugated:

avrò mangiato / I will have eaten
avrai mangiato / you will have eaten
avrà mangiato / he, she, it will have eaten
avremo mangiato / we will have eaten
avrete mangiato / you will have eaten
avranno mangiato / they will have eaten

sarò andato (-a) / I will have gone
sarai andato (-a) / you will have gone
sarà andato (-a) / he, she, it will have gone
saremo andati (-e) / we will have gone
sarete andati (-e) / you will have gone
saranno andati (-e) / they will have gone

- As you can see, this tense is rendered by the corresponding future perfect in English ("I will have eaten," etc.). It is used to express an action that occurred before a simple future action.

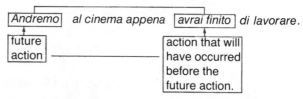

Andremo *al cinema appena* avrai finito *di lavorare.*

We will go to the movies as soon as you (will) have finished working.

- Thus, like the pluperfect, you will find it mainly in time clauses (see §8.2–5).

- In ordinary spoken Italian, there is a tendency to replace it with the simple future in temporal clauses.

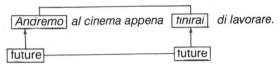

- It is also used to express probability (see §8.2–6) as in the following examples:

> *Quanto è costato il tuo orologio?* / How much did your watch cost?
> *Sarà costato centomila lire.* / It must have cost a hundred thousand lira.
> *A che ora ha telefonato?* / At what time did he phone?
> *Avrà telefonato alle sei.* / He must have phoned at six.

§8.3 THE IMPERATIVE

The imperative mood allows you to express commands and give advice. The only imperative tense is the present. You cannot command someone in the past!

- The imperative is formed by dropping the infinitive ending of the verb and adding the appropriate endings. There is, of course, no first person singular form. Note that the distinction between verbs conjugated with or without the -*isc*- (in the third conjugation) is once again applicable (see §8.2–1).

	Person	Endings		
		1st Conjugation = are	2nd Conjugation = ere	3rd Conjugation = ire
S i n g u l a r	1st	—	—	—
	2nd	-a	-i	(-isc-)-i
	3rd	-i	-a	-(isc-)-a
P l u r a l	1st	-iamo	-iamo	-iamo
	2nd	-ate	-ete	-ite
	3rd	-ino	-ano	(-isc-)-ano

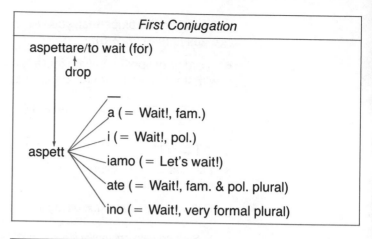

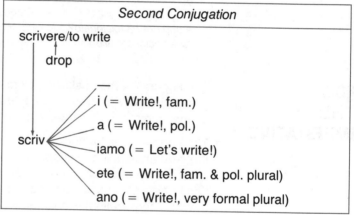

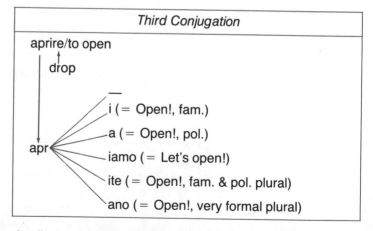

- As discussed in the previous chapter (see §7.3–1 and §7.3–2), the plural of both the familiar and polite forms tends to be the second person plural in this case as well. The third person plural is used rarely, being reserved for very formal situations.

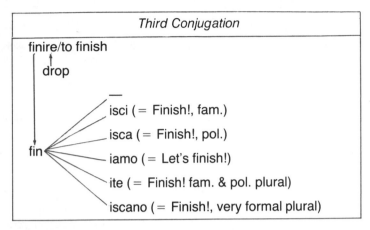

Third Conjugation
finire/to finish

drop

fin
- isci (= Finish!, fam.)
- isca (= Finish!, pol.)
- iamo (= Let's finish!)
- ite (= Finish! fam. & pol. plural)
- iscano (= Finish!, very formal plural)

EXAMPLES

Giovanni, aspetta qui! / John, wait here!

Signora Binni, scriva il Suo nome qui. / Mrs. Binni, write your name here.

Gino, Maria, andiamo a un ristorante! / Gino, Mary, let's go to a restaurant!

Aprite i vostri libri a pagina 4. / Open your books at page 4.

Signora Binni e Signor Binni, aspettate qui! / Mrs. Binni and Mr. Binni, wait here!

● As in the case of the present indicative (see §8.2–1), the hard *c* and hard *g* sounds of first conjugation verbs are retained by adding an *h* in front of the *-i, -iamo,* and *-ino* endings. And the *i* of such verbs as *cominciare* (to begin) and *mangiare* (to eat) is not repeated in front of these endings.

EXAMPLES

Signor Dini, cerchi i Suoi occhiali, per favore. / Mr. Dini, look for your glasses, please!

Paghiamo il conto! / Let's pay the bill!

Signori, paghino il conto, per favore! / Gentlemen, pay the bill, please!

Signora, cominci per favore! / Madam, please begin!

E ora, mangiamo! / And now, let's eat!

● To form the negative imperative, add *non* in the usual way (see §2.2–2). But you must make one change: the second person singular becomes the infinitive of the verb.

EXAMPLES

Affirmative	Negative
2nd Person Singular	
Aspetta! / Wait!	*Non aspettare!* / Don't wait!
Scrivi! / Write!	*Non scrivere!* / Don't write!
Paga! / Pay!	*Non pagare!* / Don't pay!

Other Persons

Aspetti! / Wait! (pol.)   *Non aspetti!* / Don't wait!
Scriviamo! / Let's write!   *Non scriviamo!* / Let's not write!
Finite! / Finish!   *Non finite ora!* / Don't finish
                                          now!

- As pointed out in the previous chapter (see §7.3–2), the object pronouns are attached to the first and second person singular and plural forms. They are not attached to the polite forms.

EXAMPLES

Polite Forms

Signor Binni, mi parli! / Mr. Binni, speak to me!
Signora Dini, gliela scriva! / Mrs. Dini, write it to him!
Signori, ce li mandino! / Gentlemen, send them to us!

Other Forms

Giovanni, parlami! / John, speak to me!
Maria, Scrivigliela! / Mary, write it to him!
Ragazzi, mandateceli! / Boys, send them to us!

- The second person singular imperative forms of *dare* (to give), *dire* (to say), *fare* (to do, to make), *andare* (to go), and *stare* (to stay) are written with an apostrophe: *da', di', fa', va',* and *sta',* respectively (see the "Verb Charts" section). When you attach the object pronouns to these forms, then you must double the first letter.

EXAMPLES

Da' la penna |a me| ! / Give me the pen!

Dammi la penna! / Give the pen to me!

Fa' |quel favore | a noi| ! / Do us that favor!

Faccelo! / Do it for us!

Di' la verità |a Maria| ! / Tell Mary the truth!

Dille la verità! / Tell her the truth!

- There is, of course, no double *gl*.

Digli la verità. / Tell him the truth.
Fagliela! / Do it for him!

- All the object pronoun patterns discussed so far apply as well to the reflexive pronouns (see §8.7).

- Recall that in the second person singular, the negative imperative form is the infinitive. With this form, the object pronouns can either be attached or put before.

EXAMPLES

Affirmative	Negative
Mangialo! / Eat it!	*Non mangiarlo!* OR *Non lo mangiare!* / Don't eat it!
Scrivimela! / Write it to me!	*Non scrivermela!* OR *Non me la scrivere!* / Don't write it to me!

§8.4 THE CONDITIONAL TENSES

The conditional mood allows you to express a condition: "I *would* go, if . . ."; "We *would* do it, but . . . ," etc. It corresponds to the English conditional and is used in exactly the same way.

§8.4 – 1 Present

The present conditional is formed in the same manner as the future (review §8.2–6).

- Drop the final -e of all three infinitives and add the appropriate set of endings to all three conjugations. Remember to change the a of the first conjugation (*are*) to e (parlar → parler).

	Person	Endings for all Three Conjugations
Singular	1st	-ei
	2nd	-esti
	3rd	-ebbe
Plural	1st	-emmo
	2nd	-este
	3rd	-ebbero

First Conjugation

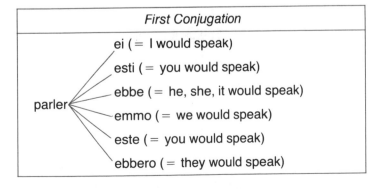

parler

ei (= I would speak)
esti (= you would speak)
ebbe (= he, she, it would speak)
emmo (= we would speak)
este (= you would speak)
ebbero (= they would speak)

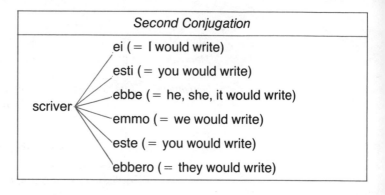

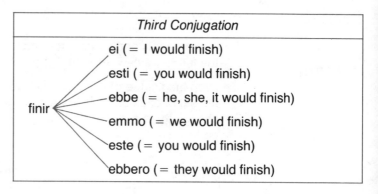

- The patterns used in the future for retaining the hard *c* and *g* sounds and writing the corresponding soft sounds in the first conjugation, apply in exactly the same way to the conditional. So go over §8.2–6 thoroughly.

EXAMPLES

Pagherei il conto, ma non ho soldi. / I would pay the bill, but I don't have any money.

Mangerebbe di più, ma non ha più tempo. / He would eat more, but he has no more time.

§8.4 – 2
Past

The past conditional is a compound tense (see §8.2–2).

- In this case, the auxiliary verb is in the present conditional.

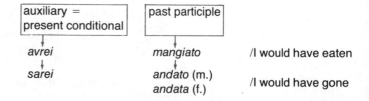

● Here are these two verbs fully conjugated:

avrei mangiato / I would have eaten
avresti mangiato / you would have eaten
avrebbe mangiato / he, she, it would have eaten
avremmo mangiato / we would have eaten
avreste mangiato / you would have eaten
avrebbero mangiato / they would have eaten

sarei andato (-a) / I would have gone
saresti andato (-a) / you would have gone
sarebbe andato (-a) / he, she, it would have gone
saremmo andati (-e) / we would have gone
sareste andati (-e) / you would have gone
sarebbero andati (-e) / they would have gone

● The past conditional corresponds to the English past conditional ("I would have . . ."; "You would have . . .," etc.) and is used in the same way. But notice that if the main verb is in a past tense, then English does not always use it, whereas Italian does.

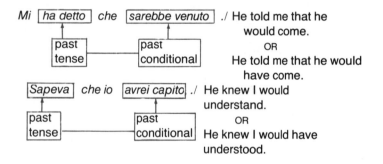

In addition, both conditional tenses are used:

—to express a polite request.
Potrei parlare? / May I speak?
—to quote someone else's opinion.
Secondo loro, quella ragazza sarebbe spagnola. / According to them, that girl is Spanish.

§8.5 THE SUBJUNCTIVE TENSES

The subjunctive mood allows you to express a point of view, fear, doubt, hope, possibility—anything that is not a fact. In a way, the subjunctive is a counterpart to the indicative, (the mood for stating facts and conveying information).

§8.5 – 1
Present

The present subjunctive is formed in the usual way by dropping the infinitive ending and attaching the following endings to the stem:

	Person	Endings		
		1st Conjugation = are	2nd Conjugation = ere	3rd Conjugation = ire
S i n g u l a r	1st	-i	-a	(-isc-)-a
	2nd	-i	-a	(-isc-)-a
	3rd	-i	-a	(-isc-)-a
P l u r a l	1st	-iamo	-iamo	-iamo
	2nd	-iate	-iate	-iate
	3rd	-ino	-ano	(-isc-)-ano

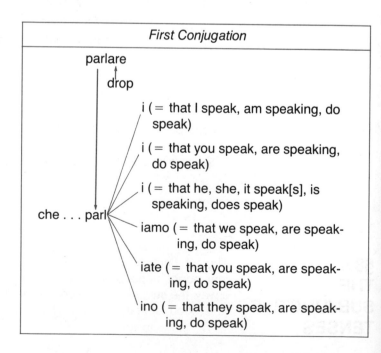

First Conjugation

parlare
↕
drop

i (= that I speak, am speaking, do speak)

i (= that you speak, are speaking, do speak)

i (= that he, she, it speak[s], is speaking, does speak)

che . . . parl

iamo (= that we speak, are speaking, do speak)

iate (= that you speak, are speaking, do speak)

ino (= that they speak, are speaking, do speak)

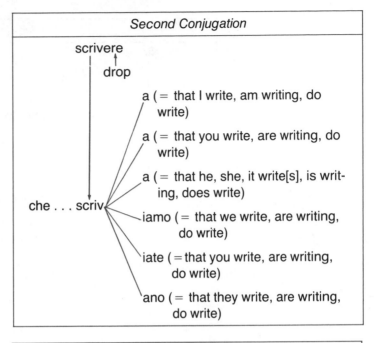

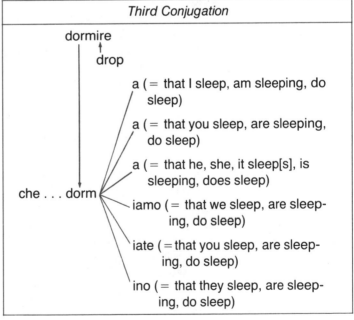

- Because the endings are often the same, you will need to use the subject pronouns with the subjunctive.

> *Sembra che tu dica la verità.* / It seems that you are telling the truth.
>
> *Sembra che lei dica la verità.* / It seems that she is telling the truth.

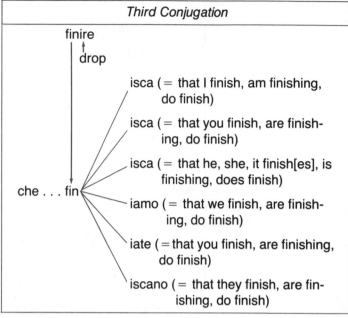

Third Conjugation

finire
↕
drop

che . . . fin →
- isca (= that I finish, am finishing, do finish)
- isca (= that you finish, are finishing, do finish)
- isca (= that he, she, it finish[es], is finishing, does finish)
- iamo (= that we finish, are finishing, do finish)
- iate (= that you finish, are finishing, do finish)
- iscano (= that they finish, are finishing, do finish)

- Notice that in the third conjugation, we find once again the distinction between verbs conjugated with the *-isc-* and those without it (see §8.2–1).

- Also applicable to this tense is the pattern of retaining the hard *c* and hard *g* sounds, and of not repeating the *i* of verbs such as *cominciare* and *mangiare*, in the first conjugation (see §8.2–1). In this case, the *h* is used before all endings (since they begin with *i*).

  Vogliamo che lui paghi il conto. / We want him to pay the bill.
  Sembra che tu mangi troppo. / It seems that you eat too much.

  The subjunctive is usually used in subordinate clauses, introduced by *che.* You will find it after a relative pronoun (see §2.3–1).

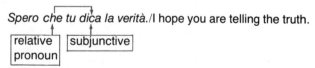

  Spero che tu dica la verità./I hope you are telling the truth.

  relative pronoun   subjunctive

- But not all verbs in relative clauses are necessarily in the subjunctive; only those connected to a main verb that expresses a nonfact (opinion, fear, supposition, anticipation, wish, hope, doubt etc.).

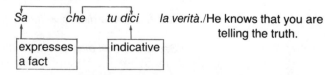

  Sa   che   tu dici   *la verità.*/He knows that you are
                                                telling the truth.

  expresses ———— indicative
  a fact

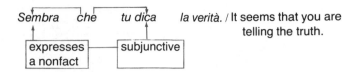

Sembra   che   tu dica   *la verità.* / It seems that you are telling the truth.

expresses a nonfact ⟶ subjunctive

- The best way to learn which of these verbs requires the subjunctive is to memorize the most commonly used ones. Here are eight of them:

credere/to believe	*pensare*/to think
desiderare/to desire	*sembrare*/to seem
dubitare/to doubt	*sperare*/to hope
immaginare/to imagine	*volere*/to want

EXAMPLES

Crede che loro arrivino stasera. / He thinks (that) they are arriving tonight.

Immagino che tu lo parli molto bene. / I imagine that you speak it very well.

Dubitano che voi finiate in tempo. / They doubt that you will finish in time.

- In current Italian, there is a tendency not to use the subjunctive in various situations. However, it is still used in writing and speaking when you want to emphasize the nonfactual nature of your thought. This is especially true when the main verb is in the negative.

Non credo che lui parli bene. / I do not think that he speaks well.

Impersonal verbs or expressions that precede the relative clause also require the subjunctive. An impersonal expression is a verb or expression that is used only in the third person.

EXAMPLES

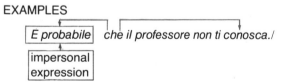

E probabile *che il professore non ti conosca.*/

impersonal expression

It's probable that the professor does not know you.

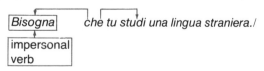

Bisogna *che tu studi una lingua straniera.*/

impersonal verb

It's necessary that you study a foreign language.

A superlative expression (review §6.5) that precedes the relative clause also requires the subjunctive.

EXAMPLES

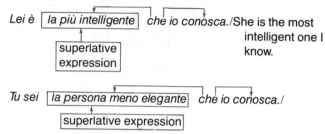

Lei è [la più intelligente] *che io conosca.*/She is the most
intelligent one I
know.

superlative
expression

Tu sei [la persona meno elegante] *che io conosca.*/

superlative expression

You are the least elegant person I know.

The subjunctive is also used after some conjunctions and
indefinite pronouns.

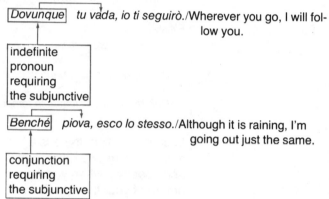

[Dovunque] *tu vada, io ti seguirò.*/Wherever you go, I will follow you.

indefinite
pronoun
requiring
the subjunctive

[Benché] *piova, esco lo stesso.*/Although it is raining, I'm
going out just the same.

conjunction
requiring
the subjunctive

● The most commonly used indefinite pronouns and conjunctions that require the subjunctive are:

Indefinite Pronouns
chiunque/whoever
dovunque/wherever
qualsiasi cosa, qualunque cosa/whatever

Conjunctions
affinché/so that
benché, sebbene/although
come se/as if
nel caso che/in the case (event) that
nonostante che/despite
senza che/without
prima che/before
purché/provided that

Finally, you will need to use the subjunctive to express
wishes and exhortations. In most cases, the clause is introduced by *che*.

EXAMPLES

Che scriva lui!/Let him write!

Che mangi tutto!/Let him eat everything!

Che piova, se vuole!/Let it rain, if it wants to!
Dio (che Dio) ce la mandi buona!/God help us!

Dio lo voglia./God willing.

As you saw in the conjugation charts at the beginning of this section, the present subjunctive has the same English equivalents as the present indicative. In other words, the present subjunctive expresses a present action with respect to the main verb.

Pare che lui dica la verità./It seems that he is telling the truth.

present action in the indicative	present action in the subjunctive

§8.5 – 2
Past

The past subjunctive is also a compound tense (review §8.2–2).

● In this case, the auxiliary verb is in the present subjunctive.

auxiliary = present subjunctive	past participle
che . . . abbia	mangiato/that I ate, have eaten, did eat
che . . . sia	andato (m.) andata (f.)/that I went, have gone

● For the present subjunctive of the auxiliary verbs, just look them up in the "Verb Charts" section of this book.

EXAMPLES

Sono contenta lui che abbia capito tutto. / I am happy that he understood everything.

Non è possibile che loro siano già partiti. / It's not possible that they have already left.

Benché sia venuto, non era felice. / Although he came, he wasn't happy.

● Notice that the past subjunctive has the same English equivalents as the present perfect (see §8.2–2). In other words, it normally expresses a past action with respect to the main verb:

Sono contenta   che lui abbia capito tutto.

present action	past action: i.e., it occurred before the main verb's action

- In other cases, the action occurred at the same time as the action of the main verb.

Benché sia venuto,   *non era felice.*

past action ——————————————— past action

- The past subjunctive is used, of course, in all of the constructions described in §8.5–1.

§8.5 – 3
Imperfect

The imperfect subjunctive is formed in the normal way by dropping the infinitive endings and attaching the following endings to the stem:

	Person	Endings to be Added		
		1st Conjugation = are	**2nd Conjugation = ere**	**3rd Conjugation = ire**
S i n g u l a r	1st	-assi	-essi	-issi
	2nd	-assi	-essi	-issi
	3rd	-asse	-esse	-isse
P l u r a l	1st	-assimo	-essimo	-issimo
	2nd	-aste	-este	-iste
	3rd	-assero	-essero	-issero

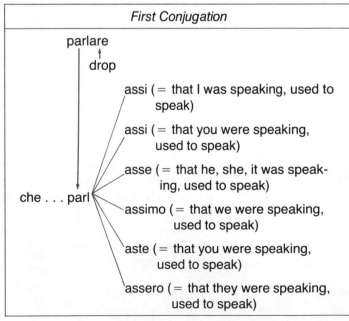

First Conjugation

parlare
↑
drop

che . . . parl

assi (= that I was speaking, used to speak)
assi (= that you were speaking, used to speak)
asse (= that he, she, it was speaking, used to speak)
assimo (= that we were speaking, used to speak)
aste (= that you were speaking, used to speak)
assero (= that they were speaking, used to speak)

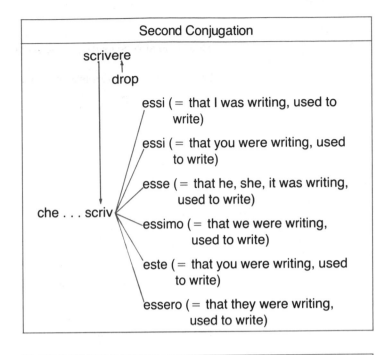

Second Conjugation		
scrivere ↑ drop		
che . . . scriv	essi (= that I was writing, used to write)	
	essi (= that you were writing, used to write)	
	esse (= that he, she, it was writing, used to write)	
	essimo (= that we were writing, used to write)	
	este (= that you were writing, used to write)	
	essero (= that they were writing, used to write)	

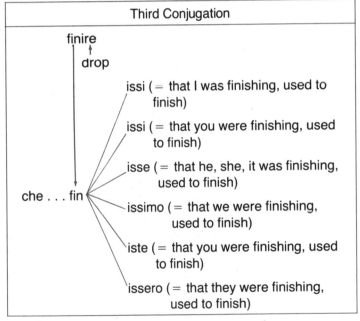

Third Conjugation		
finire ↑ drop		
che . . . fin	issi (= that I was finishing, used to finish)	
	issi (= that you were finishing, used to finish)	
	isse (= that he, she, it was finishing, used to finish)	
	issimo (= that we were finishing, used to finish)	
	iste (= that you were finishing, used to finish)	
	issero (= that they were finishing, used to finish)	

As you can see from the charts, the imperfect subjunctive has the exact same English equivalents as the imperfect indicative (see §8.2–3) and is thus used in similar ways. The only difference is that you will find it in the normal subjunctive constructions described above in §8.5–1.

EXAMPLES

Mi è sembrato che lui dicesse la verità. / It seemed to me that he
was telling the truth.

Lei era la persona più intelligente che io conoscessi. / She was
the most intelligent person I knew.

Benché piovesse ieri, sono uscito lo stesso. / Although it was
raining yester-
day, I went out
just the same.

- In other words, it is normally hooked up to a main verb in a past tense expressing an action that occurred at the same time:

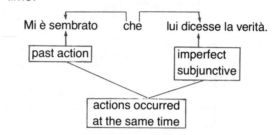

- The imperfect subjunctive is also used after *se* (if) in hypothetical clauses (see §2.3–2) when the main verb is in the conditional (present or past).

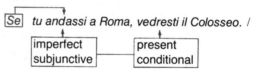

If you were to go to Rome, you would see the Colosseum.

- The imperfect subjunctive is also used in sentences expressing a wish or desire beginning with *Magari . . . !*

Magari non piovesse!/If only it wouldn't rain!

Magari venissero!/If only they would come!

§8.5 – 4
Pluperfect

The pluperfect subjunctive is a compound tense (see §8.2–2).

- In this case, the auxiliary verb is in the imperfect subjunctive.

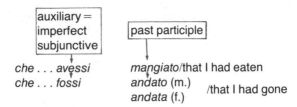

- You can look up the imperfect subjunctive of *essere* in the "Verb Charts" section of this book.

- This tense corresponds exactly to the pluperfect indicative (see §8.2–5), being used, of course, in the subjunctive constructions discussed in §8.5–1.

  EXAMPLES
  > *Mi è sembrato che lui avesse detto la verità.* / It seemed to me that he had told the truth.
  > *Eravamo contenti che foste già venuti.* / We were glad that you (pl) had already come.
  > *Benché avesse piovuto, sono uscito lo stesso.* / Although it had rained, I went out just the same.

- In other words, the pluperfect subjunctive allows you to express a past action that occurred before another past action in the subjunctive mood.

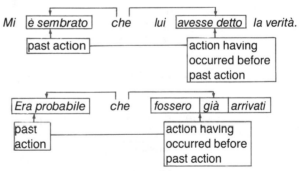

- As in the case of the imperfect subjunctive (see §8.5–3), the pluperfect is used after *se* when the main verb is in the conditional.

  EXAMPLES

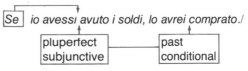

If I had had the money, I would have bought it.

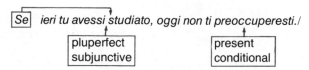

Se ieri tu avessi studiato, oggi non ti preoccuperesti./

| pluperfect subjunctive | present conditional |

If you had studied yesterday, you wouldn't worry today.

● In most speech situations, the *imperfect subjunctive* is used in conjunction with the *present conditional*, and the *pluperfect subjunctive* with the *past conditional* after *se*.

*Se avessi i soldi, lo comprerei./*If I had money, I would buy it.

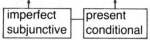

| imperfect subjunctive | present conditional |

*Se avessi avuto i soldi, lo avrei comprato./*If I had had money, I would have bought it.

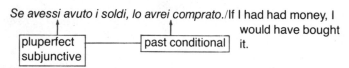

| pluperfect subjunctive | past conditional |

§8.6
THE INDEFI-
NITE TENSES

The indefinite tenses express actions that do not have the usual reference to time relationships (present, past, etc.). The time thus expressed is indefinite.

§8.6 – 1
The Infinitive

Recall from §8.1 of this chapter that there are three types of infinitives. Actually, there is a fourth type ending in *-rre*, but there are not too many infinitives of this type:

produrre / to produce
tradurre / to translate
porre / to put, place
trarre / to pull

● All verbs of this type are irregular when conjugated.

● There is also a *past infinitive* consisting of an auxiliary verb in the infinitive and a past participle.

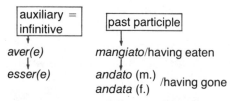

| auxiliary = infinitive | past participle |

aver(e)   *mangiato*/having eaten

esser(e)   *andato* (m.)
                 andata (f.) /having gone

● The final *-e* is normally dropped in this construction.

EXAMPLES

Dopo aver mangiato, uscirò. / After having eaten, I will go out.
Dopo esser arrivati, sono andati al cinema. / After having arrived, they went to the movies.

- The infinitive is also the only verb form used as the subject *or* the object of a preposition. It is always masculine.

  Il mangiare è necessario per vivere. / Eating is necessary in order to live.
  Invece di mangiare il vitello, ho mangiato il pollo. / Instead of eating veal, I ate chicken.

- Recall that object pronouns are normally attached to infinitives (review §7.3–2):

  Invece di mangiarlo, ho mangiato il pollo. / Instead of eating it (veal), I ate chicken.

- The infinitive is also used with verbs that require the subjunctive, when the subjects of both clauses are the same.

  Lui pensa che io parli bene./He thinks that I speak well.

  different subjects

  Lui pensa che parli bene./He thinks that he speaks well.

  same subject

  Lui pensa di parlare bene.

- For the use of prepositions in this type of construction see §10.3.

§8.6 – 2
The Gerund

The *gerund* is formed by dropping the infinitive endings and adding the following endings to the stem.

parlare	*scrivere*	*dormire*
drop	drop	drop
parlando/speaking	*scrivendo*/writing	*dormendo*/sleeping

The most important use of the gerund is in the progressive tenses, which are made up of the verb *stare* plus the gerund. The main progressive tenses in Italian are:

Present Progressive

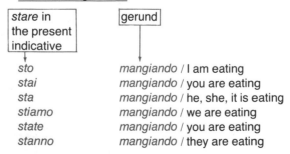

stare in the present indicative | gerund

sto	*mangiando* / I am eating
stai	*mangiando* / you are eating
sta	*mangiando* / he, she, it is eating
stiamo	*mangiando* / we are eating
state	*mangiando* / you are eating
stanno	*mangiando* / they are eating

Imperfect Progressive

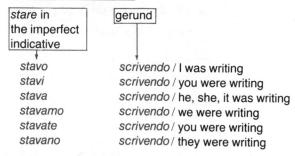

stare in the imperfect indicative	gerund
stavo	scrivendo / I was writing
stavi	scrivendo / you were writing
stava	scrivendo / he, she, it was writing
stavamo	scrivendo / we were writing
stavate	scrivendo / you were writing
stavano	scrivendo / they were writing

- As you can see, these tenses correspond exactly to the English progressive tenses, which, as you may recall, are also covered by the present indicative (see §8.2–1) and the imperfect indicative (see §8.2–3):

```
              parlo
I speak   | I am speaking |   I do speak
                 |
            sto parlando
```

```
              parlavo
| I was speaking |   I used to speak
        |
   stavo parlando
```

- Although such tenses are equivalent to the present and imperfect indicative referring to progressive action, they do give a more precise rendition of ongoing action.

- There are subjunctive counterparts to these two tenses.
  EXAMPLES
  Penso che Maria stia mangiando. / I think (that) Mary is eating.
  Pensavo che Maria stesse mangiando. / I thought that Mary was eating.

- Look up *stare* in the "Verb Charts" section for its subjunctive forms.

- The gerund can be used alone, as in English, to express an indefinite action, replacing *mentre* + imperfect indicative when the subject of the clauses is the same.
  EXAMPLES

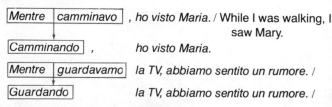

| Mentre | camminavo | , ho visto Maria. / While I was walking, I saw Mary. |
| Camminando | , | ho visto Maria. |

| Mentre | guardavamo | la TV, abbiamo sentito un rumore. / |
| Guardando | | la TV, abbiamo sentito un rumore. / |

While watching TV, we heard a noise.

- Recall that object pronouns are attached to the gerund (review §7.3–2):

  > *Guardandola, abbiamo sentito un rumore.* / Watching it (TV), we heard a noise.

- There is also a *past gerund* consisting of an auxiliary in the gerund and a past participle.

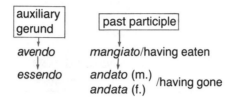

EXAMPLES

> *Avendo mangiato tutto, siamo usciti per una passeggiata.* / Having eaten everything, we went out for a stroll.
> *Essendo andati in Italia, hanno visto tante belle cose.* / Having gone to Italy, they saw many beautiful things.

§8.7 REFLEXIVE VERBS

A *reflexive* verb is simply a verb in any tense or mood that requires reflexive pronouns (review §7.2–3). A reflexive verb is identified in its infinitive form by the ending -*si* (oneself) attached to the infinitive.

> *lavarsi*/to wash oneself, *divertirsi*/to enjoy oneself, etc.

- To conjugate any reflexive verb, drop the -*si* and conjugate it as you would any verb, using, of course, the reflexive pronouns.

EXAMPLES

> *Mi lavo ogni mattina.* / I wash (myself) every morning.
> *Ci divertiremo in Italia.* / We will enjoy ourselves in Italy.
> *Sembra che tu ti diverta in Italia.* / It seems that you enjoy yourself in Italy.

- In compound tenses (see §8.2–2), all reflexive verbs are conjugated with *essere* as the auxiliary.

EXAMPLES

> *Ci siamo divertiti in Italia.* / We enjoyed ourselves in Italy.
> *Benché si fossero divertiti molto, sono ritornati presto.* / Although they had enjoyed themselves a lot, they came back early.

- Here is a list of common reflexive verbs (some of which are not reflexive in English):

> *alzarsi* / to get up, wake up; to stand up
> *annoiarsi* / to become bored
> *arrabbiarsi* / to become angry
> *dimenticarsi* / to forget
> *divertirsi* / to enjoy oneself
> *lamentarsi* / to complain
> *lavarsi* / to wash (oneself)
> *mettersi* (a) / to begin to, set about; to wear
> *prepararsi* / to prepare oneself
> *sentirsi* / to feel
> *sposarsi* / to marry
> *svegliarsi* / to wake up
> *vergognarsi* / to be ashamed

- Recall that, in the imperative, the pronouns are attached to the "nonpolite" forms (see §8.3).

EXAMPLES

Lavati! / Wash yourself!
Sposiamoci! / Let's get married!
Non arrabbiatevi! / Dont get angry!

BUT

Si lavi! / Wash yourself! (pol.)
Non Si arrabbi! / Don't get angry! (pol.)

- In compound tenses, the past participle of reflexive verbs agrees with the direct object pronouns (*lo, la, li, le*), even if otherwise it normally agrees with the subject.

EXAMPLES

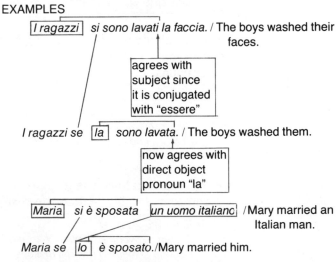

Some verbs occur in both reflexive and nonreflexive forms.

> *alzare*/to lift up; *alzarsi*/to get up
> *lavare*/to wash something; *lavarsi*/to wash oneself

Many verbs can be made reflexive by simply adding the appropriate pronouns. In such cases, the verbs are called *reciprocal*.

> *Si telefonano ogni sera.* / They phone each other every evening.
> *Ci scriviamo spesso.* / We write to each other often.

In compound tenses, these verbs are treated like any reflexive verb, and are thus conjugated with *essere*.

> *Hanno telefonato ieri sera.* / They phoned last evening.
> BUT
> *Si sono telefonati ogni sera.* / They phoned each other every evening.

§8.8 THE PASSIVE VOICE

Up to this point, all the verbs have been described in their active form. But any verb can be easily turned into its corresponding passive form by the following formula. Review the concepts of *active* and *passive* in §2.2–5:

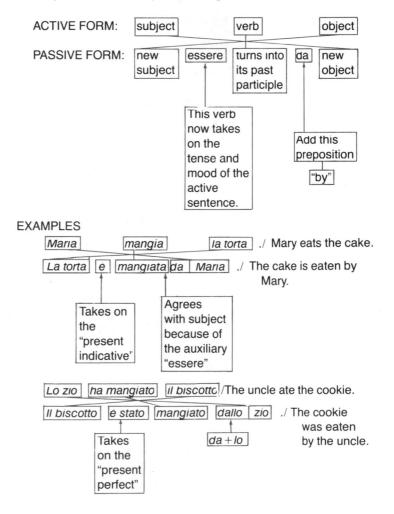

EXAMPLES

• The passive can be found in subjunctive constructions as well.

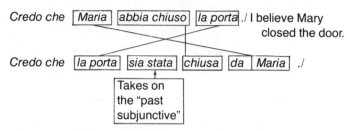

I believe the door was closed by Mary.

The main *modal* verbs of Italian are *potere* (to be able to), *dovere* (to have to), and *volere* (to want). You can look up their irregular forms in the "Verb Charts" section. A modal verb is simply one that is normally followed by an infinitive.

EXAMPLES

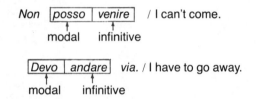

Modal verbs have the following characteristics:

• In compound tenses (§8.2–2), the auxiliary verb is determined by the infinitive.

• However, in current conversational Italian, there is a tendency to use only *avere* as the auxiliary.

Ho voluto uscire./I wanted to go out.

• Recall that object pronouns can be put before the modal verb, or attached to the infinitive (§7.3–2):

La voglio mangiare. / I want to eat it.

OR

Voglio mangiarla.

- Be careful! In compound tenses, the past participle of the modal agrees with the direct object pronoun *if* the object precedes the past participle.

  *Ho voluto mangiarla./*I wanted to eat it.

                    BUT

  La no voluta mangiare.

- In the case of reflexive verbs, used in modal construction, note the following:

  > If the reflexive pronoun is attached to the infinitive, then the auxiliary is *avere* in compound tenses, and there is no agreement.

  *Maria non ha potuto divertirsi./*Mary was not able to enjoy herself.

reflexive pronoun attached to its infinitive

  > But if the reflexive pronoun is put before the modal, then *essere* is used, and there is agreement.

  *Maria non si è potuta divertire./*Mary was not able to enjoy herself.

reflexive pronoun comes before

- When put into the conditional, these verbs are translated as "could," "would," "should" (present conditional) and as "could have," "would have," "should have" (past conditional).

  Lo potrei fare. / I could do it.
  L'avrei potuto fare. / I could have done it.

  Lo dovrei fare. / I should do it.
  L'avrei dovuto fare. / I should have done it.

  Lo vonei fare. / I would like to do it.
  L'avrei voluto fare. / I would like to have done it.

§9.

Adverbs

Adverbs are words that modify verbs, adjectives, or other adverbs. They indicate quantity, time, place, degree of intensity, and manner.

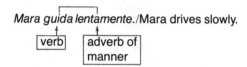

Mara guida lentamente./Mara drives slowly.

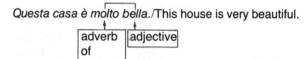

Questa casa è molto bella./This house is very beautiful.

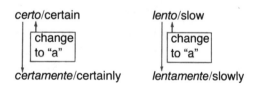

Giovanni guida troppo lentamente./John drives too slowly.

§9.2 ADVERBS OF MANNER

Adverbs of manner are formed in the following ways. Notice that the ending *-mente* corresponds to the English ending "-ly."

● Change a descriptive adjective ending in *-o* (see §6.2) to *-a*, and add *-mente*.

certo/certain   *lento*/slow

change to "a"   change to "a"

certamente/certainly   *lentamente*/slowly

● If the adjective ends in *-e* (see §6.2), then simply add on *-mente*.

elegante / elegant + *-mente* = *elegantemente* / elegantly
semplice / simple + *-mente* = *semplicemente* / simply

● However, if the adjective ends in *-le* or *-re* and is preceded by a vowel, then you must drop the *-e*.

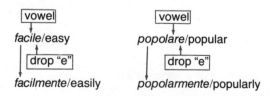

vowel   vowel

facile/easy   *popolare*/popular

drop "e"   drop "e"

facilmente/easily   *popolarmente*/popularly

- The exceptions to these rules are *benevolo* (benevolent) → *benevolmente* (benevolently), *leggero* (light) → *leggermente* (lightly), and *violento* (violent) → *violentemente* (violently).

EXAMPLES

Adjective	Adverb of Manner
raro / rare	*raramente* / rarely
vero / true	*veramente* / truly
preciso / precise	*precisamente* / precisely
felice / happy	*felicemente* / happily
triste / sad	*tristemente* / sadly
enorme / enormous	*enormemente* / enormously
speciale / special	*specialmente* / specially
utile / useful	*utilmente* / usefully
regolare / regular	*regolarmente* / regularly

- These adverbs normally follow the verb, but they may begin a sentence for emphasis.

EXAMPLES

Lui scrive ai suoi parenti regolarmente. / He writes to his relatives regularly.

Regolarmente, lui scrive ai suoi parenti. / Regularly, he writes to his relatives.

§9.3 OTHER KINDS OF ADVERBS

Here are some important adverbs you will need for ordinary conversation.

abbastanza/enough	*oggi*/today
allora/then	*oggigiorno*/nowadays
anche/also, too	*ormai*/by now
ancora/still, yet	*per caso*/by chance
anzi/as a matter of fact	*piuttosto*/rather
appena/just (have done something)	*poi*/then (eventually)
bene/well	*presto*/early
di nuovo, ancora/again	*prima*/first
domani/tomorrow	*purtroppo*/unfortunately
finora/until now	*quasi*/almost
fra poco/in a little while	*qui*/here
già/already	*solo*/only
in fretta/in a hurry	*stamani*/this morning
insieme/together	*stasera*/this evening
invece/instead	*subito*/right away
lì, là/there	*tardi*/late
male/bad(ly)	*vicino*/near(by)
nel frattempo/in the meanwhile	

EXAMPLES

Noi andiamo spesso al cinema. / We often go to the movies.
Ripeti quello che hai detto ancora una volta. / Repeat what you have said once more.

Sono quasi le tre. / It is almost three o'clock.

- As in English, adverbs are normally placed after a verb. In compound tenses (see §8.2–2), many adverbs can be put between the auxiliary verb and the past participle.

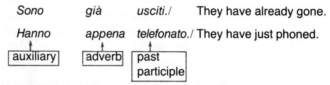

| *Sono* | *già* | *usciti.*/ | They have already gone. |
| *Hanno* | *appena* | *telefonato.*/ | They have just phoned. |

auxiliary   adverb   past participle

- However, this cannot be done with all adverbs, as is the case in English (which has the same patterns for positioning adverbs).

- The adjectives *molto, tanto, poco, troppo, parecchio* (see §6.4–4) are adverbs as well. In this case, be careful! There is no *noun* for them to agree with!

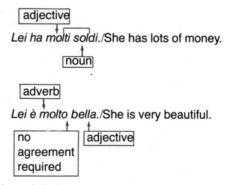

adjective
Lei ha molti soldi./She has lots of money.
noun

adverb
Lei è molto bella./She is very beautiful.
no agreement required   adjective

- You might have trouble with expressions that use nouns in Italian but adjectives in English. These are listed in §13.2.

Italian	English
Lui ha molta fame.	He is very hungry.
noun.	adjective

§9.4 THE COMPARISON OF ADVERBS

Adverbs are compared in exactly the same way as adjectives. So review §6.5.

EXAMPLES

lentamente/slowly ⟶ *più lentamente*/more slowly
vicino/near ⟶ *meno vicino*/less near
lontano/far ⟶ *il più lontano*/the farthest

● Notice the following equivalences:

> *bene*/well→*più bene* = *meglio*/better→*il più bene* =
> *il meglio*/the best
>
> *male*/bad(ly)→*più male* = *peggio*/worse→*il più male*
> = *il peggio*/the worst

● Given that both the adjectives *buono* and *cattivo* and their corresponding adverbs *bene* and *male* are rendered in English by "better" and "worse," respectively, you might become confused about which form to use. Here is a guideline for you:

better = *migliore* or *meglio*?
To figure out which form to use, just go back to the "noncompared" form of the sentence: That wine is better. (compared form)   That wine is good. (noncompared form)   You can now see that it is an adjective.   Therefore, you must use the adjective form *migliore*.   *Quel vino è migliore.*/That wine is better.
That watch works better. (compared form)   That watch works well. (noncompared form)   You can now see that it is an adverb.   Therefore, you must use the adverb form *meglio*.   *Quell'orologio funziona meglio.*/That watch works better.
Use exactly the same method for *peggiore* and *peggio*.

§10.

Prepositions

§10.1
WHAT ARE
PREPOSI-
TIONS?

Prepositions (literally, "a word that comes before") are words that come before another word or phrase to show its relationship to some other part in the sentence.

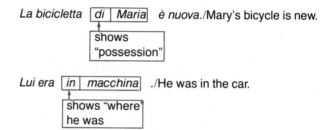

La bicicletta di Maria *è nuova.*/Mary's bicycle is new.

shows "possession"

Lui era in macchina ./He was in the car.

shows "where" he was

§10.2
PREPOSI-
TIONAL
CONTRAC-
TIONS

When the prepositions *a* (to, at), *di* (of), *da* (from), *su* (on), and *in* (in) immediately precede a definite article (review §4.2–1), they contract with it to form one word.

Questo è il romanzo del professore ./This is the professor's novel.

di + il

C'è una lira nella scatola ./There's a lira in the box.

in + la

Vengo dall' Italia ./I come from Italy.

da + l'

The following chart summarizes the different contractions:

	lo	l'	gli	il	i	la	le
a	allo	all'	agli	al	ai	alla	alle
di	dello	dell'	degli	del	dei	della	delle
da	dallo	dall'	dagli	dal	dai	dalla	dalle
su	sullo	sull'	sugli	sul	sui	sulla	sulle
in	nello	nell	negli	nel	nei	nella	nelle

EXAMPLES

I gioielli sono nel cassetto. / The jewels are in the drawer.
Ecco le matite degli studenti. / Here are the students' pencils.
Le forchette sono sulla tavola. / The forks are on the table.

- The preposition *con* (with) also contracts frequently with the *l'* and *il* forms, although this is not obligatory.

  EXAMPLES

  > `con + l' = coll'`

  Nadia viene coll'avvocato di Paolo. / Nadia is coming with Paul's lawyer.

  OR

  Nadia viene con l'avvocato di Paolo.

  > `con + il = col`

  Claudia parla col direttore generale. / Ciaudia is speaking with the manager.

  OR

  Claudia parla con il direttore.

- Other prepositions do not contract. Some common ones are *per* (through, on account of), *tra (fra)* (between, among), *sopra* (above), *sotto* (below).

  EXAMPLES

  Lo faccio per il principio. / I'm doing it on (account of) principle.
  L'ho messo tra la tavola e la sedia. / I put it between the table and the chair.

- There are some compound prepositions as well, that is, prepositions made up of two words.

  EXAMPLES

  È vicino alla camera. / It is near the bedroom.
  Sono davanti alla finestra. / I'm in front of the window.

- The prepositions do not contract with the indefinite article.

  EXAMPLES

  L'ho messo in un cassetto. / I put it in a drawer.
  È l'orologio di una donna ricca. / It's the watch of a rich woman.

- The article may be dropped after the preposition in some frequently used expressions.

  EXAMPLES

  Sono a casa. / I'm at home.
  Vado in macchina. / I'm going by car.

- However, when the noun is modified in some way, then the article *must* be used.

  Sono alla casa nuova di Roberto. / I'm at Robert's new house.
  Vado nella macchina verde di Luigi. / I'm going in Louis' green car.

§10.3
SOME USES

Prepositions have many, many uses, and all of them cannot possibly be mentioned here. But here are a few important ones for you to remember:

A is used with a city to express "in."
Abito a Roma./I live in Rome.
Otherwise *in* is used:
Abito in Italia.

Di is used to show possession or relationship:

È l'esame del professore./It is the professor's exam.
È la figlia di Maria./She is Mary's daughter.

Da is used not only to express "from" but also "to" in expressions such as:

to the doctor's	at the pharmacist's	at Mary's
dal dottore	*dal farmacista*	*da Maria*

It translates "since" and "for" in time expressions:

I have been living here	since	Monday.
Abito qui	*da*	*lunedì.*

I have been living here	for	three days.
Abito qui	*da*	*tre giorni.*

It translates the expression "as a . . ."

Te lo dico da amico./I'm telling you as a friend.
Da piccolo, suonavo il flauto./As a young child, I used to play the flute.

It is used in expressions made up of noun + infinitive or noun + noun:

una macchina da vendere/a car to sell
vestito da sera/evening dress

Per is used in time expressions, rather than *da*, when "future duration" is implied:

I will live in this city	for	three years.
Abiterò in questa città	*per*	*tre anni.*

- There are three ways to translate "to" between a conjugated verb and an infinitive.

- Some verbs are followed by *a*.

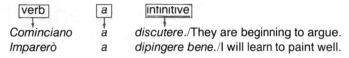

| *Cominciano* | a | *discutere.*/They are beginning to argue. |
| *Imparerò* | a | *dipingere bene.*/I will learn to paint well. |

- Some verbs are followed by *di*.

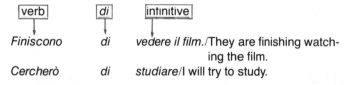

| *Finiscono* | di | *vedere il film.*/They are finishing watching the film. |
| *Cercherò* | di | *studiare*/I will try to study. |

Modal verbs (see §8.9), as well as a few other verbs, do not require a preposition.

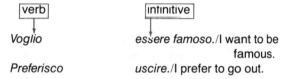

| *Voglio* | *essere famoso.*/I want to be famous. |
| *Preferisco* | *uscire.*/I prefer to go out. |

- The only way to learn which preposition (if any) is appropriate in such expressions is to memorize the preposition along with the verb by consulting a dictionary.

§11.

Negatives and Other Grammatical Points

§11.1
WHAT ARE
NEGATIVES?

Negatives are words that allow you to say something in the negative.

Non conosco nessuno. / I do not know anyone.
Non lo faccio più. / I won't do it anymore.

§11.2
COMMON
NEGATIVES

Recall that any sentence can be made negative in Italian by simply putting *non* before the predicate (see §2.1–2). The following are some common negative constructions:

---

non . . . mai/never
non . . . nessuno/no one
non . . . niente, nulla/nothing
non . . . più/no more, no longer
non . . . neanche, nemmeno, neppure/not even
non . . . né . . . né/neither . . . nor
non . . . mica/not . . . really

EXAMPLES

Positive	Negative
Canto sempre. / I always sing.	*Non canto mai.* / I never sing.
Qualcuno grida. / Someone is shouting.	*Non grida nessuno.* / No one is shouting.
Lo faccio spesso. / I do it often.	*Non lo faccio più.* / I do not do it anymore.

- You can put a negative at the beginning of a sentence if you wish to be more emphatic. In this case, you drop the *non*.

EXAMPLES

Nessuno parla! / No one is speaking!
Mai capirò i verbi! / Never will I understand verbs!

§11.3
OTHER
GRAMMAT-
ICAL POINTS

The conjunctions *e* (and) and *o* (or) allow you to join similar things (two nouns, two verbs, two phrases, etc.).

Marco e Carlo sono amici./Mark and Charles are friends.
noun   noun

Uno studia all'università e *l'altro lavora in fabbrica* /
     sentence   sentence

One studies at the university, and the other works in a factory.

- The conjunction *e* and the preposition *a* word can be changed to *ed* and *ad*, respectively, before a noun or adjective beginning with a vowel. This makes the pronunciation smoother.

Gina ed Elena sono buone amiche./Gina and Helen are good
    ↑   friends.
vowel

Abito ad Atene./I live in Athens.
       ↑
      vowel

Be careful with the following common expressions!

Singular	Plural
Che cosa è?/What is it?	*Che cosa sono?*/What are they?
È un libro./It is a book.	*Sono dei libri.*/They are books.
Che cosa c'è qui?/What is here?	*Ci sono foto qui?*/Are there photographs here?
C'è una foto qui./There is a photograph here.	*Sì, ci sono alcune foto.*/Yes, there are some photographs here.
Dov'è il ristorante?/Where is the restaurant?	*Dove sono i ristoranti?*/Where are the restaurants?
Ecco l'indirizzo./Here (there) is the address.	*Ecco gli indirizzi.*/Here (there) are the addresses.

- The form *ecco* is invariable; but in the other expressions the verb can, of course, be in any tense and mood:

Sarà un ristorante. / It must be a restaurant.
C'erano due foto sulla tavola. / There were two photographs on
                                          the table.

The verb *fare* can be used to render "to have/get something done" and "to have/get someone to do something." Such expressions are called *causative*. The most common form of causative construction is as follows. (Notice how it differs from English).

subject	"fare"	+ infinitive	object(s)	
Maria	*fa*	*lavare*	*i piatti*	*a suo fratello.*
Mary	is having	her brother	wash	the dishes.

- Object pronouns can, of course, be used in a causative construction.

- As with all verbs, the pronouns are attached in the imperative and indefinite tenses.

EXAMPLES

Faglieli lavare! / Have him wash them!
Vuole farglieli lavare. / She wants to have him wash them.

- There are, of course, other ways to form this construction. However, the one above is the most basic. The others are derived from it.

Special Topics

§12.

The Verb *Piacere*

**§12.1
EXPRESSING
"TO LIKE"**

The verb *piacere* allows you to express what you like in Italian. But it is a tricky verb because it really means "to be pleasing to."

**§12.2
CHARACTER-
ISTICS**

Piacere is conjugated irregularly in several tenses. You will find its conjugation in the "Verb Charts" section of this book.

● In order to use this verb correctly, you must always think of what it *really* means.

| Mi | piace | quella gonna. |
| That skirt | is pleasing | to me | . = I like that skirt.

| Mi | piacciono | quelle gonne | .
| Those skirts | are pleasing | to me | . = I like those skirts.

● If you think in this way, you will always be correct. Notice that with indirect object pronouns, the real subject is usually put at the end (although this is not necessary).

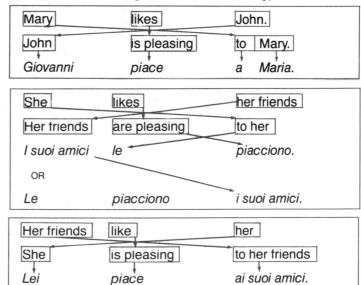

Mary	likes	John.
John	is pleasing	to	Mary.
Giovanni	piace	a	Maria.

She	likes	her friends
Her friends	are pleasing	to her
I suoi amici	le	piacciono.
	OR	
Le	piacciono	i suoi amici.

Her friends	like	her
She	is pleasing	to her friends
Lei	piace	ai suoi amici.

- Be careful using the following expressions!

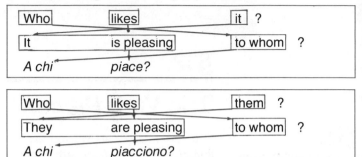

- In compound tenses (see §8.2–2), *piacere* is conjugated with *essere* (to be). This means, of course, that the past participle agrees with the subject—no matter where you put it.

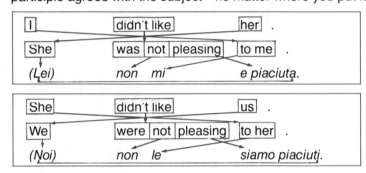

- And do not forget that you might need to use those object pronouns that come after the verb for reasons of emphasis or clarity.

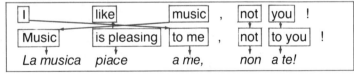

§12.3
A HANDY
RULE OF
THUMB

As you can see, this can be very confusing for anyone accustomed to the English verb "to like." The following rule of thumb might help you use this important verb more readily:

> Since the verb is often used with indirect object pronouns, just think of the pronouns as *subjects*; then make the verb agree with the predicate!

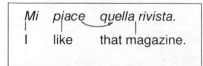

(lit., That magazine is pleasing to me.)

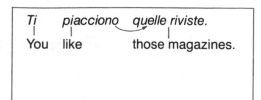

Ti   piacciono   quelle riviste.
You   like   those magazines.

(lit., Those
magazines are
pleasing to
you.)

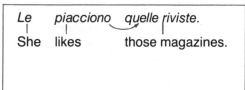

Gli   piace   quella rivista.
He   likes   that magazine.

(lit., That magazine is
pleasing to him.)

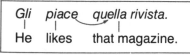

Le   piacciono   quelle riviste.
She   likes   those magazines.

(lit., Those
magazines are
pleasing to
her.)

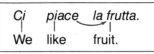

Ci   piace   la frutta.
We   like   fruit.

(lit., Fruit is pleasing to us.)

Vi   piacciono i formaggi italiani.
You   like   Italian cheeses.

(lit., Italian
cheeses are
pleasing to you.)

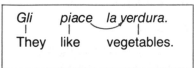

Gli   piace   la verdura.
They   like   vegetables.

(lit., Vegetables are
pleasing to them.)

- Remember: this is merely a rule of thumb. If you are
  unsure, you must go through the procedure described in
  §12.2.

§12.4 EXPRESSING "DISLIKE"

To say that you do not like something, simply put *non* before
the predicate in the normal fashion (review §2.2–2).

> *Non mi piace quella rivista.* / I do not like that magazine.
> *Non le piacciono i ravioli.* / She doesn't like ravioli.

- Be careful! The verb *dispiacere* is not used to express the
  same thing. This verb is used in the following ways,
  together with an indirect object pronoun.

> *Mi dispiace.*/I'm sorry.
> *Ti dispiace.*/You are sorry.
> *Gli dispiace.*/He is sorry.
> etc.

Idiomatic Expressions

§13.1
WHAT ARE
IDIOMATIC
EXPRES-
SIONS?

§13.2
EXPRES-
SIONS WITH
AVERE

An idiomatic expression is a phrase that is fixed in form and whose meaning cannot always be determined by the meanings of the particular words in the expression. For example, the English expression "He kicked the bucket" cannot be altered in any way; otherwise, it would lose its meaning.

The following expressions are made up of *avere* + noun, whereas their English equivalents are made up of "to be" + adjective.

	ho	*fame.*
literally	I have	hunger.
meaning	I am hungry.	

Here is a list of important idioms:

> *avere fame*/to be hungry
> *avere sete*/to be thirsty
>
> *avere caldo*/to be hot
> *avere freddo*/to be cold
>
> *avere sonno*/to be sleepy
>
> *avere ragione*/to be right
> *avere torto*/to be wrong
>
> *avere fretta*/to be in a hurry
>
> *avere paura*/to be afraid
>
> *avere vergogna*/to be ashamed

EXAMPLES
> *Ieri avevamo fame e allora abbiamo mangiato molto.* / Yesterday we were hungry, so we ate a lot.
> *Scusa, ma ho fretta.* / Excuse me, but I'm in a hurry.
> *Penso che tu abbia torto.* / I think you are wrong.

Here are a few other expressions with *avere:*

> *avere voglia (di)*/to feel like
> *avere bisogno (di)*/to need
> *avercela con qualcuno*/to be angry with someone
> *avere l'occasione (di)*/to have the opportunity to

EXAMPLES

Stasera, non ho voglia di uscire. / Tonight, I don't feel like going out.

Gli studenti hanno bisogno di tanta pazienza. / Students need a lot of patience.

Perché ce l'hai con Franca? / Why are you angry with Franca?

§13.3 EXPRES- SIONS WITH *FARE, DARE,* AND *STARE*

If you do not know how to conjugate these irregular verbs, just look them up in the "Verb Charts" section of this book.

Expressions with *Fare*
fare a meno di/to do without *fare attenzione a*/to pay attention to *fare finta di*/to pretend *fare il biglietto*/to buy a (transportation) ticket *farsi la barba*/to shave *fare una domanda a*/to ask a question *fare una passeggiata*/to go for a walk *fare senza*/to do without *farsi vivo*/to show up *Faccia pure!*/Go ahead! (Please do!) *Faccio io!*/I'll do it! *Non fa niente!*/It doesn't matter! *Non fa per me.*/It doesn't suit me.

EXAMPLES

Ho fatto il biglietto con Alitalia. / I bought my ticket from Alitalia.

Ogni mattina mi faccio la barba. / Every morning I shave.

Giovanni, perché non ti fai mai vivo? / John, why don't you come (show up) more often?

With *Dare*
darsi da fare/to get busy *dare fastidio a*/to bother (someone) *dare la mano a*/to shake hands *dare retta a*/to heed (pay attention to)

EXAMPLES

Il fumo mi dà fastidio. / Smoke bothers me.

Dare la mano a qualcuno è un segno di cortesia. / Shaking someone's hand is a sign of courtesy.

Da' retta a me! / Heed what I say!

With *Stare*
stare a qualcuno (+ infinitive)/to be up to someone *stare per*/to be about to *stare zitto*/to be quiet *Come sta?* (pol.)/*Come stai* (fam.)?/How are you? *Sto bene.*/I am well.

EXAMPLES

Giorgio, sta' zitto! / George, be quiet!
Sta alla signora Rossi scrivere. / It's up to Mrs. Rossi to write.
Ieri stavo per uscire, quando sono arrivati alcuni amici. / Yesterday I was about to go out, when some friends arrived.

§13.4
MISCELLA-
NEOUS
EXPRES-
SIONS

a destra/to the right *a sinistra*/to the left *nord, sud, est, ovest*/north, south, east, west *Ti piace? Altro che!*/Do you like it? I'll say! *a lungo andare*/in the long run *valere la pena (di)*/to be worthwhile *Auguri!*/All the best! or Congratulations! *in ogni caso*/in any case *Che guaio!*/What a mess! *Non ne posso più!*/I can't stand it anymore! *prendere in giro*/to pull one's leg *Ci vuole molto tempo.*/It will take a long time. *Lo ha fatto apposta!*/He did it on purpose! *Che combinazione!*/What a coincidence! *dipendere da*/to depend on *qualcosa di buono*/something good *niente di buono*/nothing good

EXAMPLES

Quel negozio è qui, a destra. / That store is here, to the right.
Davvero? Non mi prendere in giro! / Really? Don't pull my leg!
Tutto dipende da te. / Everything depends on you.

§14.

Numbers

Cardinal numbers are used for counting (*one, two, three,* etc.) *Ordinal* numbers are used to indicate order (*first, second, third*, etc.).

The numbers from zero to twenty:

Zero to twenty			
0	*zero*	11	*undici*
		12	*dodici*
1	*uno*	13	*tredici*
2	*due*	14	*quattordici*
3	*tre*	15	*quindici*
4	*quattro*	16	*sedici*
5	*cinque*	17	*diciassette*
6	*sei*	18	*diciotto*
7	*sette*	19	*diciannove*
8	*otto*	20	*venti*
9	*nove*		
10	*dieci*		

The numbers from twenty on are formed by adding the first nine numbers to each new category of tens, keeping the following adjustments in mind:

- In front of *uno* and *otto* (the only two that start with a vowel), drop the final vowel of the tens number:

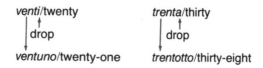

venti/twenty
↑
|drop
↓
ventuno/twenty-one

trenta/thirty
↑
|drop
↓
trentotto/thirty-eight

- When *tre* is added on, it must be written with an accent:

venti + tre = venti*trè*
trenta + tre = trenta*trè*

Twenty to a hundred		
20 venti	30 trenta	70 settanta
21 ventuno	31 trentuno	71 settantuno
22 ventidue	32 trentadue	72 settantadue
23 ventitrè	...	...
24 ventiquattro	40 quaranta	
25 venticinque	41 quarantuno	80 ottanta
26 ventisei	42 quarantadue	81 ottantuno
27 ventisette	...	82 ottantadue
28 ventotto	50 cinquanta	...
29 ventinove	51 cinquantuno	90 novanta
	52 cinquantadue	91 novantuno
	...	92 novantadue
	60 sessanta	...
	61 sessantuno	100 cento
	62 sessantadue	
	...	

The same method of construction applies to the remaining numbers:

Numbers above a hundred		
	1000 mille	100.000 centomila
101 centuno	1001 milleuno	200.000 duecentomila
102 centodue	retain the "e"	...
...		1.000.000 un milione
200 duecento	1002 milledue	2.000.000 due milioni
300 trecento	...	...
...	2000 duemila	1.000.000.000 un miliardo
900 novecento	3000 tremila	
...		

- Notice that the plural of *mille* is *mila*, whereas *un milione* and *un miliardo* are pluralized in the normal way (see §3.3–1).

  EXAMPLES
  due milioni / two million
  tre miliardi / three billion

- The other numbers are invariable, except *uno/una*, as noted below.
- Cardinal numbers normally are placed before a noun.

  EXAMPLES
  tre persone / three persons
  cinquantotto minuti / fifty-eight minutes

- When you put *uno* (or any number constructed with it, e.g., *ventuno, trentuno*, etc.) before a noun, then you must treat it exactly like the indefinite article (see §4.2–2).

EXAMPLES

uno zio / one uncle
ventun anni / twenty-one years
trentun giorni / thirty-one days

- *Milione* (*-i*) and *miliardo* (*-i*) are always followed by *di* before a noun.

EXAMPLES

un milione di dollari / a million dollars
due milioni di abitanti / two million inhabitants
tre miliardi di lire / three thousand lira

- The cardinal numbers may be written as one word. But for large numbers, you may need to separate them logically so they can be read easily.

30.256 = trentamila duecento cinquantasei
(rather than: *trentamiladuecentocinquantasei*!)

§14.3 The Ordinal Numbers

The first ten ordinal numbers are:

First to tenth			
1st	*primo*	6th	*sesto*
2nd	*secondo*	7th	*settimo*
3rd	*terzo*	8th	*ottavo*
4th	*quarto*	9th	*nono*
5th	*quinto*	10th	*decimo*

The remaining ordinal numbers are easily constructed in the following manner.

- Take the corresponding cardinal number, drop its vowel ending, and then add *-esimo*.

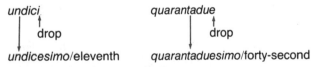

undici   *quarantadue*
    drop   drop
undicesimo/eleventh   *quarantaduesimo*/forty-second

- In the case of numbers ending in *trè*, remove the accent mark (in writing), but keep the final *e*.

ventitrè + *esimo* = *ventitreesimo*/twenty-third
trentatrè + *esimo* = *trentatreesimo*/thirty-third

- Unlike the cardinal numbers, ordinals are adjectives that precede the noun. Therefore, they agree with the noun in the normal fashion (see §6.2).

EXAMPLES

il primo giorno / the first day
la ventesima volta / the twentieth time
gli ottavi capitoli / the eighth chapters

- As any adjective, they can be easily transformed into a pronoun (see §7.2).

  È il quinto che ho fatto. / It's the fifth one I have done.

- As in English, ordinals are used to express the denominator of fractions, whereas the numerator is expressed by cardinals.

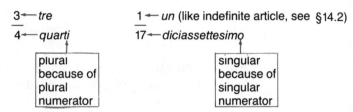

$$\frac{3 \leftarrow tre}{4 \leftarrow quarti}$$

plural because of plural numerator

$1 \leftarrow un$ (like indefinite article, see §14.2)

$17 \leftarrow diciassettesimo$

singular because of singular numerator

- Be careful! ½ = *mezzo/metà*
- The definite article is not used before an ordinal and a proper name.

  EXAMPLES

  Papa Giovanni XXIII (= ventitreesimo) / Pope John (the) XXIII
  Luigi XIV (= quattordicesimo) / Louis (the) XIV

§14.4 NUMERICAL EXPRES- SIONS

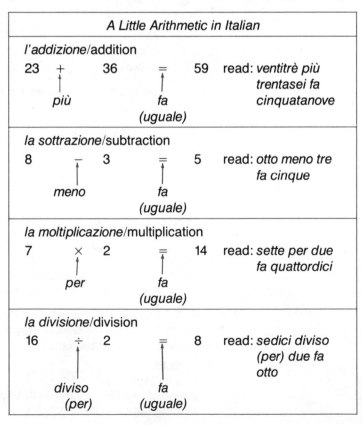

A Little Arithmetic in Italian
l'addizione/addition
23 + 36 = 59   read: *ventitrè più*
↑   ↑   *trentasei fa*
più   *fa*   *cinquatanove*
(uguale)
la sottrazione/subtraction
8 − 3 = 5   read: *otto meno tre*
↑   ↑   *fa cinque*
meno   *fa*
(uguale)
la moltiplicazione/multiplication
7 × 2 = 14   read: *sette per due*
↑   ↑   *fa quattordici*
per   *fa*
(uguale)
la divisione/division
16 ÷ 2 = 8   read: *sedici diviso*
(per) due fa
otto
diviso   *fa*
(per)   *(uguale)*

How Old Are You?

Quanti anni hai? (fam.)/How old are you?
Quanti anni ha? (pol.)/How old are you?

Ho ventidue anni./I'm twenty-two years old.

> literally,
> "I have 22 years."

Ho trentanove anni./I'm thirty-nine years old.

> literally,
> "I have 39 years."

Some Expressions

il doppio/double
a due a due, a tre a tre . . . /two by two, three by
three . . .

una dozzina/a dozen
una ventina, una trentina . . . /about twenty, about
thirty . . .

un centinaio/about a hundred
due centinaia, tre centinaia . . ./about two hundred,
about three
hundred . . .

un migliaio/about a thousand
due migliaia, tre migliaia . . ./about two thousand,
about three thou-
sand . . .

§15.

Telling Time

You can ask this question either in the singular:
Che ora è?

or in the plural:
Che ore sono?

- The word *ora* literally means "hour." The abstract concept of "time" is expressed by *il tempo.*

    Come passa il tempo! / How time flies!

- The hours are all feminine. Therefore, they are preceded by the feminine forms of the definite article (see §4.2–1):

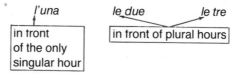

l'una
in front of the only singular hour

le due *le tre*
in front of plural hours

- Do not forget to make your verbs and prepositions agree!

Che ora è?

È l'una./It's one o'clock.

Sono le due. Sono le tre./It's two o'clock. It's three o'clock.

A che ora arriverai?/At what time are you arriving?
All'una./At one o'clock.
Alle due. Alle tre./At two o'clock. At three o'clock.

● In ordinary conversation, morning, afternoon, and evening hours are distinguished by the following expressions:

> *di mattina (della mattina)*/in the morning
> *di sera (della sera)*/in the evening (afternoon)
> *di notte (della notte)*/in the /at night

> *Sono le otto di mattina.* / It's eight o'clock in the morning.
> *Sono le cinque di sera.* / It's five o'clock in the afternoon
> (evening).

● Although *pomeriggio* means "afternoon," in most parts of Italy, *sera* is used to refer to P.M.

● Officially, Italian time works on the basis of the twenty-four hour clock. Thus, after noon (*le dodici*), official hours are as follows:

EXAMPLES
> *Sono le quindici.* / It's 3 P.M.
> *Sono le venti.* / It's 8 P.M.
> *Sono le ventiquattro.* / It's (twelve) midnight.

§15.3 Minutes

Minutes (*i minuti*) are simply added to the hour with the conjunction *e* (and).

EXAMPLES
> *Sono le tre e venti* / It's three-twenty.
> *Sono le quattro e dieci.* / It's ten after four.
> *È l'una e quaranta.* / It's one-forty.
> *Sono le sedici e cinquanta* / It's 4:50 P.M.
> *Sono le ventidue e cinque.* / It's 10:05 P.M.

- As the next hour approaches, an alternative way of expressing the minutes is: the next hour *minus* the number of minutes left to go.

  8:58 = *le otto e cinquantotto*

  OR

  le nove meno due (nine minus two)

  10:50 = *le dieci e cinquanta*

  OR

  le undici meno dieci (eleven minus ten)

- The expressions *un quarto* (a quarter), and *mezzo/mezza* also can express the quarter hour and the half hour.

  3:15 = *le tre e quindici*

  OR

  le tre e un quarto

  4:30 = *le quattro e trenta*

  OR

  le quattro e mezzo/mezza

  5:45 = *le sei meno quindici*

  OR

  le sei meno un quarto

  OR

  le cinque e tre quarti (three and three quarters)

§15.4 TIME EXPRES- SIONS

Here are some useful time expressions:

noon/midday: *le dodici* OR *mezzogiorno* midnight: *le ventiquattro* OR *mezzanotte* EXAMPLES *È mezzogiorno e venti.*/It's twelve-twenty. (noon) *È mezzanotte e mezzo.*/It's twelve-thirty. (midnight)

il secondo/second	*l'orologio va avanti*/fast
l'orologio/watch or clock	watch
la sveglia/alarm clock	*l'orologio va indietro*/slow
il quadrante/dial	watch
le lancette/hands (of a clock)	*precisa(-e)*/on the dot
l'orario/schedule	(*l'una precisa* or *le due precise*)

§16.

Days, Months, Seasons, Dates, and the Weather

You can ask this question in one of two main ways:

Che data è (oggi)?
OR
Quanti ne abbiamo oggi?

The latter one literally means "How many of them (= days) do we have?" Thus, you are asking for the "number" of the day, and that is the response you will get.

Che data è?
È il tre maggio. (or È il tre.) / It's May third. (or It's the third.)

OR
Quanti ne abbiamo oggi? / It's May third.
(Ne abbiamo) tre.

I giorni della settimana are:

lunedì/Monday	*venerdì*/Friday
martedì/Tuesday	*sabato*/Saturday
mercoledì/Wednesday	*domenica*/Sunday
giovedì/Thursday	

- The days are all masculine, except for *domenica*, which is feminine.

- The expression "On Mondays, Tuesdays," etc., is expressed in Italian with the definite article.

EXAMPLES
il martedì / on Tuesdays
il sabato / on Saturdays
la domenica / on Sundays

- Notice that the days are not capitalized (unless, of course, they are the first word of a sentence).

I mesi dell'anno are:

gennaio/January	*luglio*/July
febbraio/February	*agosto*/August
marzo/March	*settembre*/September
aprile/April	*ottobre*/October
maggio/May	*novembre*/November
giugno/June	*dicembre*/December

- The months are not capitalized (unless they are the first word of a sentence).

- The preposition *di* is often used with a month to indicate something habitual or permanent.

  EXAMPLES

  > *Di febbraio andiamo spesso al mare.* / Every February we often go to the sea (beach).
  >
  > *Di maggio c'è sempre tanto sole.* / Every may there is always lots of sunshine.

  Note: *Ogni* may be used in place of *di*: *ogni febbraio* . . .

- The preposition *a* is used to indicate when something will take place.

  EXAMPLES

  > *Verrò a giugno.* / I will come in June.
  >
  > *Torneranno a luglio.* / They will return in July.

- The preposition *tra (fra)* is used to indicate "in how much time."

  EXAMPLES

  > *Maria andrà in Italia tra due mesi.* / Mary is going to Italy in two months' time.
  >
  > *Arriveremo fra otto ore.* / We will arrive in eight hours' time.

§16.4 SEASONS

Le stagioni dell'anno are as follows:

la primavera/spring	*l'autunno*/fall
l'estate/summer	*l'inverno*/winter

§16.5 RELATED EXPRESSIONS

Here are some useful expressions:

prossimo (-a)/next: *la settimana prossima*/next week; *il mese prossimo*/next month
scorso (-a)/last: *la settimana scorsa*/last week; *il mese scorso*/last month
due giorni fa, tre mesi fa, un anno fa . . ./two days ago, three months ago, a year ago . . .
a domani, a giovedì . . ./till tomorrow, till Thursday . . . *domani a otto, domenica a otto* . . ./a week from tomorrow, a week from Sunday . . .
il giorno/the day: *la giornata*/the whole day (long) *la sera*/the evening: *la serata*/the whole evening (long)

oggi/today
ieri/yesterday
domani/tomorrow
avantieri/the day before yesterday
dopodomani/the day after tomorrow

§16.6 DATES

Dates are expressed by the following formula:

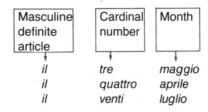

Masculine definite article	Cardinal number	Month
il	tre	maggio
il	quattro	aprile
il	venti	luglio

EXAMPLES

Oggi è il ventinove gennaio. / Today is January 29.
Oggi è il quindici settembre. / Today is September 15.
Oggi è lunedì, il sedici marzo. / Today is Monday, March 16.
Oggi è mercoledì, il due dicembre. / Today is Wednesday, December 2.

- The exception to this is the first day of every month, for which you must use the ordinal number *primo*.

  È il primo ottobre. / It's October 1.
  È il primo giugno. / It's June 1.

Years are always preceded by the definite article.

EXAMPLES

È il 1984./It's 1984.
Sono nato nel 1946./I was born in 1946.

in + *il*

- However, in complete dates, the article is omitted before the year.

  Oggi è il cinque febbraio, 1985. / Today is February 5, 1985.

§16.7 THE WEATHER

Che tempo fa? (How's the weather?)
Fa bel tempo./It's beautiful (weather).
Fa brutto (cattivo) tempo./It's bad (awful) weather.
Fa caldo./It's hot.
Fa freddo./It's cold.
Fa molto caldo (freddo)./It's very hot (cold).
Fa un po' caldo (freddo)./It's a bit hot (cold).
Fa fresco./It's cool.
Il caldo è insopportabile./The heat is unbearable.

Le previsioni del tempo (The weather forecast)
Piove./It is raining. *Nevica.*/It is snowing. *Tira vento.*/It is windy. *È nuvoloso.*/It is cloudy. *la pioggia*/rain *la neve*/snow *il vento*/wind *la grandine*/hail *l'alba*/dawn *il tramonto*/twilight *il temporale*/storm *il tuono*/clap of thunder (verb: *tuonare*) *il lampo*/flash of lightning (verb: *lampeggiare*)

- Keep in mind that you can express the weather in the past or in the future.

  EXAMPLES

  Ieri pioveva. / Yesterday it was raining.
  Domani nevicherà. / Tomorrow it will snow.
  Ieri faceva molto freddo. / Yesterday it was very cold.
  Quest'anno ha fatto bel tempo. / This year the weather has been beautiful.

- When referring to climate in general, use *essere*.

  In Italia il tempo è sempre bello. / The weather is always beautiful in Italy.

§17.

Common Conversation Techniques

§17.1 WHAT ARE CONVERSATION TECHNIQUES?

Conversation technique is the manner in which you use a word, phrase, sentence, or expression to communicate within a given situation. Knowing how to start a conversation, how to express politeness, how to ask for something — each is a situation that requires knowledge of appropriate vocabulary and expressions. By knowing how to use the parts of speech, you already know quite a bit about how to communicate: you need interrogative adjectives to ask all kinds of questions; imperative verb forms to give commands; subjunctive tenses to express opinion, doubt, wishes, etc. However, there are some expressions that are not easily classifiable in this way. The following are only a few very common ones.

§17.2 STARTING AND ENDING CONVERSATIONS

Saying Hello		
Buon giorno, *Buona sera,*	*signor Verdi,* *signora Verdi,* *signorina Verdi,*	*come va?*
Hello,	Mr. Verdi, Mrs. Verdi, Miss Verdi,	how's it going?

- In polite address, "hello" is expressed as *buon giorno* (good morning) until noon, and as *buona sera* (good evening, afternoon) from noon on. These words can also be written as one word: *buongiorno, buonasera.*

Ciao,	*Marco,*	*come va?*
Hi,	Mark,	how's it going?

- In familiar address, *ciao* (hi) is used at any time of the day.

Responding		
Bene,	*grazie*	*e Lei?*
Non c'e male,		*e tu?*
Well,	thank you,	and you?
Not bad,		

Making a Phone Call			
Pronto.	*Con chi parlo?*		
	C'e	*il signor . . ./la signora . . ./la signorina . . .?*	
		Marco?	
Hello.	With whom am I speaking?		
	Is	Mr. . . ./Mrs. . . ./Miss . . ./there?	
		Mark there?	

Answering a Phone Call		
Pronto.	*Chi parla?*	*Sì, sono . . .*
Hello.	Who is it?	Yes, this is . . .

Ending Conversations/Phone Calls
Buon giorno.   *Buona sera.*   *Ciao.*
Good-bye.

- The expressions used to start conversations are also used to end them. In addition, you might say *arrivederci* (polite: *arrivederLa*); *buona notte* (good night); *a presto* (see you soon); *a più tardi* (see you later).

- When approached by waiters, store clerks, etc., you will often hear:

Desidera? (sing.)
Desiderano? (pl.)
May I help you?

§17.3 INTRODUCING PEOPLE

Come si chiama, Lei? (pol.)	*Mi chiamo . . .*
Come ti chiami? (fam.)	
What is your name?	My name is . . .

Le presento/Permette che Le presenti . . . (pol.)
Ti presento/Permetti che ti presenti . . . (fam.)
Allow me to introduce you to . . .

Piacere di fare	*la Sua conoscenza.* (pol.)
	la tua conoscenza. (fam.)
A pleasure to make	your acquaintance.

§17.4 BEING POLITE

Scusi. (pol.) *Scusa.* (fam.)
Permesso. (used when making one's way through people)
Excuse me.

Grazie.	*mille.* *tante.*	*Prego.*
Thank you	very much.	You're welcome.

Avanti, si accomodi.
Come in, make yourself comfortable.

Buon appetito!	*Salute!*
used at meals (lit, Have a good appetite!)	Cheers!

§17.5 EXPRESSING YOUR FEELINGS

Surprise
Vero? *Davvero?* *No!* ————— Really?
Come? ————————— How come?
Scherza? (pol.) *Scherzi?* (fam.) ——— Are you joking?
Incredibile! ————— Unbelievable or Incredible!

Agreement/Disagreement
Buon' idea. ————— Good idea.
D'accordo. *Va bene.* ————— OK.
Non va bene. ————— It's not OK.
Non sono d'accordo. ——— I do not agree.

Pity/Resignation	
Peccato.	Too bad./It's a pity.
Mi dispiace.	I'm sorry.
Che triste!	How sad!
Non c'è niente da fare.	There's nothing to do.
Pazienza!	Patience!

Indifference/Boredom	
Non importa.	It doesn't matter.
Per me è lo stesso.	It's all the same thing to me.
Fa lo stesso.	It's the same thing.
Uffa!	exclamation similar to "ugh"!
Basta!	Enough!
Che noia!	What a bore!

§18.

Synonyms and Antonyms

§18.1
WHAT ARE
SYNONYMS
AND
ANTONYMS?

Synonyms are words that have the same meaning. *Antonyms* are words that have an opposite meaning. Knowing Italian synonyms and antonyms will help you to relate words, thereby enriching your vocabulary.

§18.2
SYNONYMS

Synonyms allow you to say the same thing in a different way, thus increasing your communicative abilities. Keep in mind, however, that no two words have the exact meaning.

Meaning	Synonyms	
to ask	*chiedere*	*domandare*
crazy	*pazzo*	*matto*
dress/suit	*abito*	*vestito*
face	*faccia*	*viso*
gladly	*volentieri*	*con piacere*
much/many/a lot	*molto*	*tanto*
near	*vicino*	*presso*
nothing	*niente*	*nulla*
now	*ora*	*adesso*
only	*solo*	*solamente, soltanto*
please	*per piacere*	*per favore*
quick(ly)	*veloce(mente)*	*svelto*
the same	*lo stesso*	*uguale*
slowly	*lentamente*	*piano*

Meaning	Synonyms	
street/road	*strada*	*via*
therefore	*quindi*	*dunque, perciò*
truly/really	*veramente*	*davvero*
to understand	*capire*	*comprendere*
unfortunately	*purtroppo*	*sfortunatamente*

- The verbs *conoscere* and *sapere* both mean "to know," but are used in different ways.

> "To know someone" is rendered by *conoscere*.

EXAMPLES

Maria non conosce quell'avvocatessa. / Mary doesn't know that lawyer.
Chi conosce la dottoressa Verdi? / Who knows Dr. Verdi?

> "To know how to do something" is rendered by *sapere*.

EXAMPLES

Mia sorella non sa pattinare. / My sister doesn't know how to skate.
Sai cucire? / Do you know how to sew?

> "To know something" is normally rendered by *sapere*.

EXAMPLES

Guglielmo non sa la verità. / William doesn't know the truth.
Chi sa come si chiama quella donna? / Who knows what that woman's name is?

> "To be familiar with something" is rendered by *conoscere*.

EXAMPLES

Conosci Roma? / Are you familiar with Rome?
Conosco un bel ristorante qui vicino. / I know (= I am familiar with) a restaurant nearby.

> When referring to subjects, *sapere* implies complete knowledge, *conoscere* implies partial knowledge.

Lo sai l'italiano? / Do you know Italian?
Lo conosco. / I'm familiar with it.

§18.3
ANTONYMS

Thinking in opposites will also develop your vocabulary.

alba/sunrise	*tramonto*/sunset
alto/tall	*basso*/short
aperto/open	*chiuso*/closed
atterraggio/take-off	*decollo*/landing
bello/beautiful	*brutto*/ugly
bene/well	*male*/bad
bianco/white	*nero*/black
buono/good	*cattivo*/bad
chiaro/light	*scuro*/dark
dentro/inside	*fuori*/outside
entrata/entrance	*uscita*/exit
facile/easy	*difficile*/difficult
magro/thin	*grasso*/fat
presto/early	*tardi*/late
pulito/clean	*sporco*/dirty
piccolo/small	*grande*/big
primo/first	*ultimo*/last
ricco/rich	*povero*/poor
simpatico/nice, pleasant	*antipatico*/unpleasant, disagreeable
spesso/often	*mai*/never
tanto, molto/much	*poco*/little
trovare/to find	*perdere*/to lose
tutto/everything	*niente, nulla*/nothing
vecchio/old	*giovane*/young
vendere/to sell	*comprare*/to buy
venire/to come	*andare*/to go
vicino/near(by)	*lontano*/far
vuoto/empty	*pieno*/full

§19.

Cognates: Good and False Friends

A *cognate* is a word in Italian that looks like a word in English. This is because they have a common origin. They are, so to speak, "friends." But like all friends, they can be "good" or "false."

Cognates that have the *same* meaning are, of course, good friends. Differences between English and Italian occur in the endings of the words. Here are a few related endings that will help you take advantage of language similarities.

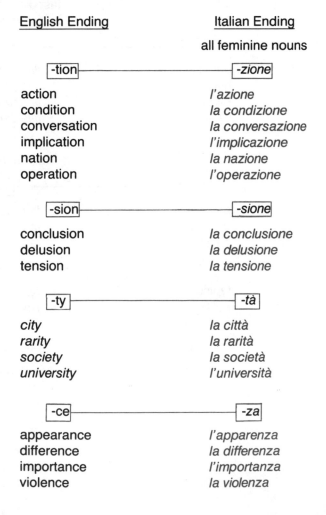

English Ending	Italian Ending
	all feminine nouns
-tion	-zione
action	l'azione
condition	la condizione
conversation	la conversazione
implication	l'implicazione
nation	la nazione
operation	l'operazione
-sion	-sione
conclusion	la conclusione
delusion	la delusione
tension	la tensione
-ty	-tà
city	la città
rarity	la rarità
society	la società
university	l'università
-ce	-za
appearance	l'apparenza
difference	la differenza
importance	l'importanza
violence	la violenza

all masculine nouns

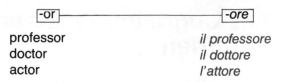

-or	-ore
professor	*il professore*
doctor	*il dottore*
actor	*l'attore*

adjectives ending in -*o*, or
masculine nouns

-ary	-ario
arbitrary	*arbitrario*
ordinary	*ordinario*
vocabulary	*il vocabolario*

masculine or feminine
nouns (see §3.2–2)

-ist	-ista
dentist	*il//la dentista*
pianist	*il//la pianista*
tourist	*il//la turista*
violinist	*il//la violinista*

all feminine nouns

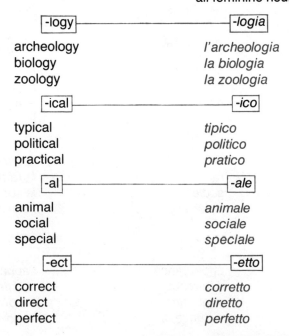

-logy	-logia
archeology	*l'archeologia*
biology	*la biologia*
zoology	*la zoologia*

-ical	-ico
typical	*tipico*
political	*politico*
practical	*pratico*

-al	-ale
animal	*animale*
social	*sociale*
special	*speciale*

-ect	-etto
correct	*corretto*
direct	*diretto*
perfect	*perfetto*

- Of course, you will also find many good friends among verbs.

English Verbs	Italian Verbs
analyze	analizzare
complicate	complicare
emigrate	emigrare
indicate	indicare
prefer	preferire

§19.3 THE FALSE FRIENDS

Cognates that do not have the same meaning are, needless to say, false friends. Here are a few very common ones:

English Word	False Friend	Correct Word
assist	assistere = to be present	aiutare
accident	accidente = unexpected event	l'incidente
brave	bravo = good, fine	coraggioso
effective	effettivo = actual	efficace
argument	argomento = topic	la discussione, la lite
conductor (musical)	conduttore = train conductor	il direttore (d'orchestra)
complexion	complessione = constitution	la carnagione
magazine	magazzino = warehouse, department store	la rivista
stamp	stampa = the press	il francobollo
sensible	sensibile = sensitive	sensato
lecture	lettura = reading	la conferenza
large	largo = wide	grande
firm	firma = signature	la ditta, l'azienda
factory	fattoria = farm	la fabbrica

English Word	False Friend	Correct Word
disgrace	*disgrazia* = misfortune	*la vergogna*
contest	*contesto* = context	*il concorso*
confront	*confrontare* = to compare	*affrontare*
parent	*parente* = relative	*il genitore*
library	*libreria* = bookstore	*la biblioteca*

- Of course, to be sure whether a cognate is a good or false friend, you will have to look it up in a dictionary.

Verb Charts

The following verbs are irregular in one or more tenses as shown. Their individual conjugations are displayed from left to right (where applicable).

EXAMPLE

Andare in the present indicative:

vado (1st person singular), vai (2nd person singular), va (3rd person singular), andiamo (1st person plural), andate (2nd person plural), vanno (3rd person plural)

andare **to go**	Present Indicative:	vado, vai, va, andiamo, andate, vanno
	Future:	andrò, andrai, andrà, andremo, andrete, andranno
	Imperative:	—— va', vada, andiamo, andate, vadano
	Present Conditional:	andrei, andresti, andrebbe, andremmo, andreste, andrebbero
	Present Subjunctive:	vada, vada, vada, andiamo, andiate, vadano
avere **to have**	Present Indicative:	ho, hai, ha, abbiamo, avete, hanno
	Past Absolute:	ebbi, avesti, ebbe, avemmo, aveste, ebbero
	Future:	avrò, avrai, avrà, avremo, avrete, avranno
	Imperative:	—— abbi, abbia, abbiamo, abbiate, abbiano
	Present Conditional:	avrei, avresti, avrebbe, avremmo, avreste, avrebbero
	Present Subjunctive:	abbia, abbia, abbia, abbiamo, abbiate, abbiano
bere **to drink**	Present Indicative:	bevo, bevi, beve, beviamo, bevete, bevono
	Past Participle:	bevuto
	Imperfect:	bevevo, bevevi, beveva, bevevamo, bevevate, bevevano
	Past Absolute:	bevvi (bevetti), bevesti, bevve (bevvette), bevemmo, beveste, bevvero (bevettero)

	Future:	berrò, berrai, berrà, berremo, berrete, berranno
	Imperative:	—— bevi, beva, beviamo, bevete, bevano
	Present Conditional:	berrei, berresti, berrebbe, berremmo, berreste, berrebbero
	Present Subjunctive:	beva, beva, beva, beviamo, beviate, bevano
	Imperfect Subjunctive:	bevessi, bevessi, bevesse, bevessimo, beveste, bevessero
	Gerund:	bevendo
cadere to fall	Past Absolute:	caddi, cadesti, cadde, cademmo, cadeste, caddero
	Future:	cadrò, cadrai, cadrà, cademo, cadrete, cadranno
	Present Conditional:	cadrei, cadresti, cadrebbe, cadremmo, cadreste, cadrebbero
	(Conjugated the same way: *accadere*/to happen)	
chiedere to ask	Past Participle:	chiesto
	Past Absolute:	chiesi, chiedesti, chiese, chiedemmo, chiedeste, chiesero
chiudere to close	Past Participle:	chiuso
	Past Absolute:	chiusi, chiudesti, chiuse, chiudemmo, chiudeste, chiusero
conoscere to know, be acquainted with (people, places)	Past Absolute:	conobbi, conoscesti, conobbe, conoscemmo, conosceste, conobbero
dare to give	Present Indicative:	do, dai, dà, diamo, date, danno
	Past Participle:	dato
	Imperfect:	davo, davi, dava, davamo, davate, davano
	Past Absolute:	diedi, desti, diede, demmo, deste, diedero
	Future:	darò, darai, darà, daremo, darete, daranno
	Imperative:	—— da', dia, diamo, date, diano
	Present Conditional:	darei, daresti, darebbe, daremmo, dareste, darebbero
	Present Subjunctive:	dia, dia, dia, diamo, diate, diano
	Imperfect Subjunctive:	dessi, dessi, desse, dessimo, deste, dessero
	Gerund:	dando

dire **to say (tell)**	Present Indicative:	dico, dici, dice, diciamo, dite, dicono
	Past Participle:	detto
	Imperfect:	dicevo, dicevi, diceva, dicevamo, dicevate, dicevano
	Past Absolute:	dissi, dicesti, disse, dicemmo, diceste, dissero
	Future:	dirò, dirai, dirà, diremo, direte, diranno
	Imperative:	—— di', dica, diciamo, dite, dicano
	Present Conditional:	direi, diresti, direbbe, diremmo, direste, direbbero
	Present Subjunctive:	dica, dica, dica, diciamo, diciate, dicano
	Imperfect Subjunctive:	dicessi, dicessi, dicesse, dicessimo, diceste, dicessero
	Gerund:	dicendo
dovere **to have to**	Present Indicative:	devo, devi, deve, dobbiamo, dovete, devono
	Future:	dovrò, dovrai, dovrà, dovremo, dovrete, dovranno
	Present Conditional:	dovrei, dovresti, dovrebbe, dovremmo, dovreste, dovrebbero
	Present Subjunctive:	deva (debba), deva (debba), deva (debba), dobbiamo, dobbiate, devano (debbano)
essere **to be**	Present Indicative:	sono, sei, è, siamo, siete, sono
	Past Participle:	stato
	Imperfect:	ero, eri, era, eravamo, eravate, erano
	Past Absolute:	fui, fosti, fu, fummo, foste, furono
	Future:	sarò, sarai, sarà, saremo, sarete, saranno
	Imperative:	—— sii, sia, siamo, siate, siano
	Present Conditional:	sarei, saresti, sarebbe, saremmo, sareste, sarebbero
	Present Subjunctive:	sia, sia, sia, siamo, siate, siano
	Imperfect Subjunctive:	fossi, fossi, fosse, fossimo, foste, fossero
fare **to do; to make**	Present Indicative:	faccio, fai, fa, facciamo, fate, fanno
	Past Participle:	fatto
	Imperfect:	facevo, facevi, faceva, facevamo, facevate, facevano
	Past Absolute:	feci, facesti, fece, facemmo, faceste, fecero

	Future:	farò, farai, farà, faremo, farete, faranno
	Imperative:	—— fa', faccia, facciamo, fate, facciano
	Present Conditional:	farei, faresti, farebbe, faremmo, fareste, farebbero
	Present Subjunctive:	faccia, faccia, facciamo, facciate, facciano
	Imperfect Subjunctive:	facessi, facessi, facesse, facessimo, faceste, facessero
	Gerund:	facendo

leggere to read	Past Participle: Past Absolute	letto lessi, leggesti, lesse, leggemmo, leggeste, lessero

mettere to put	Past Participle: Past Absolute:	messo misi, mettesti, mise, mettemmo, metteste, misero

(Conjugated the same way: *ammettere*/to admit, *commettere*/to commit, *omettere*/to omit, *permettere*/to permit, *promettere*/to promise)

nascere to be born	Past Participle: Past Absolute:	nato nacqui, nascesti, nacque, nascemmo, nasceste, nacquero

piacere to like (to be pleasing to)	Present Indicative: Past Absolute: Present Subjunctive:	piaccio, piaci, piace, piacciamo, piacete, piacciono piacqui, piacesti, piacque, piacemmo, piaceste, piacquero piaccia, piaccia, piaccia, piacciamo, piacciate, piacciano

potere to be able to	Present Indicative: Future: Present Conditional: Present Subjunctive:	posso, puoi, può, possiamo, potete, possono potrò, potrai, potrà, potremo, potrete, potranno potrei, potresti, potrebbe, potremmo, potreste, potrebbero possa, possa, possa, possiamo, possiate, possano

prendere to take	Past Participle: Past Absolute:	preso presi, prendesti, prese, prendemmo, prendeste, presero

(Conjugated the same way: *comprendere*/to comprehend, *sorprendere*/to surprise)

salire to go up, climb	Present Indicative:	salgo, sali, sale, saliamo, salite, salgono
	Imperative:	—— sali, salga, saliamo, salite, salgano
	Present Subjunctive:	salga, salga, salga, saliamo, saliate, salgano
sapere to know	Present Indicative:	so, sai, sa, sappiamo, sapete, sanno
	Past Absolute:	seppi, sapesti, seppe, sapemmo, sapeste, seppero
	Future:	saprò, saprai, saprà, sapremo, saprete, sapranno
	Present Conditional:	saprei, sapresti, saprebbe, sapremmo, sapreste, saprebbero
	Present Subjunctive:	sappia, sappia, sappia, sappiamo, sappiate, sappiano
scegliere to choose, select	Present Indicative:	scelgo, scegli, sceglie, scegliamo, scegliete, scelgono
	Past Participle:	scelto
	Past Absolute:	scelsi, scegliesti, scelse, scegliemmo, sceglieste, scelsero
	Imperative:	—— scegli, scelga, scegliamo, scegliete, scelgano
	Present Subjunctive:	scelga, scelga, scelga, scegliamo, scegliate, scelgano
scendere to descend, go down	Past Participle:	sceso
	Past Absolute:	scesi, scendesti, scese, scendemmo, scendeste, scesero
scrivere to write	Past Participle:	scritto
	Past Absolute:	scrissi, scrivesti, scrisse, scrivemmo, scriveste, scrissero
	(Conjugated the same way: descrivere/to describe, prescrivere/to prescribe)	
stare to stay, remain	Present Indicative:	sto, stai, sta, stiamo, state, stanno
	Past Participle:	stato
	Imperfect:	stavo, stavi, stava, stavamo, stavate, stavano
	Past Absolute:	stetti, stesti, stette, stemmo, steste, stettero
	Future:	starò, starai, starà, staremo, starete, staranno

	Imperative:	——, sta', stia, stiamo, state, stiano
	Present Conditional:	starei, staresti, starebbe, staremmo, stareste, starebbero
	Present Subjunctive:	stia, stia, stia, stiamo, stiate, stiano
	Imperfect Subjunctive:	stessi, stessi, stesse, stessimo, steste, stessero

tenere **to keep, to hold**	Present Indicative:	tengo, tieni, tiene, teniamo, tenete, tengono
	Past Absolute:	tenni, tenesti, tenne, tenemmo, teneste, tennero
	Future:	terrò, terrai, terrà, terremo, terrete, terranno
	Imperative:	—— tieni, tenga, teniamo, tenete, tengano
	Present Conditional:	terrei, terresti, terrebbe, terremmo, terreste, terrebbero
	Present Subjunctive:	tenga, tenga, tenga, teniamo, tenete, tengano

(Conjugated the same way: *contenere*/to contain, *mantenere*/to support someone, *ritenere*/to retain)

uscire **to go out**	Present Indicative:	esco, esci, esce, usciamo, uscite, escono
	Imperative:	—— esci, esca, usciamo, uscite, escano
	Present Subjunctive:	esca, esca, esca, usciamo, usciate, escano

vedere **to see**	Past Participle:	visto (veduto)
	Past Absolute:	vidi, vedesti, vide, vedemmo, vedeste, videro
	Future:	vedrò, vedrai, vedrà, vedremo, vedrete, vedranno
	Present Conditional:	vedrei, vedresti, vedrebbe, vedremmo, vedreste, vedrebbero

venire **to come**	Present Indicative:	vengo, vieni, viene, veniamo, venite, vengono
	Past Participle:	venuto
	Past Absolute:	venni, venisti, venne, venimmo, veniste, vennero
	Future:	verrò, verrai, verrà, verremo, verrete, verranno
	Imperative:	—— vieni, venga, veniamo, venite, vengano

	Present Conditional:	verrei, verresti, verrebbe, verremmo, verreste, verrebbero
	Present Subjunctive:	venga, venga, venga, veniamo, veniate, vengano

volere to want	Present Indicative:	voglio, vuoi, vuole, vogliamo, volete, vogliono
	Past Absolute:	volli, volesti, volle, volemmo, voleste, vollero
	Future:	vorrò, vorrai, vorrà, vorremo, vorrete, vorranno
	Present Conditional:	vorrei, vorresti, vorrebbe, vorremmo, vorreste, vorrebbero
	Present Subjunctive:	voglia, voglia, voglia, vogliamo, vogliate, vogliano

LET'S REVIEW

The vocabulary used in the following exercises and activities is found throughout the Grammar Brush-Up section (including the irregular verbs listed in the Verb Charts).

Any new vocabulary needed for the exercises is defined as it is introduced.

The exercises and activities are numbered consecutively, even though they are divided up according to the chapters in the Grammar Brush-Up section.

Test Yourself

1.
ITALIAN SOUNDS AND SPELLING

> The hard *c* and hard *g* sounds represented by *c, ch, g,* and *gh* are missing from the following words. Put the correct letter(s) in each blank.

1. __c__ ane ("dog"), __c__ ravatta ("tie"), __c__ ome ("how"), __g__ ola ("throat"), __g__ rande ("big"), spa __gh__ etti ("spaghetti"), __ch__ iesa ("church"), __gh__ iaccio ("ice")

> The soft *c* and soft *g* sounds represented by *c, ci, g,* and *gi* are missing from the following words. Put the correct letter(s) in each blank.

2. __ci__ ao ("hi, bye"), __gi__ orno ("day"), __c__ ena ("dinner"), __g__ iro ("turn"), __ci__ occolata ("chocolate"), __g__ ente ("people"), __c__ inema ("movies"), __gi__ acca ("jacket")

> The following words are misspelled. Correct them.

3. scerzo ("joke") _____ , schena ("scene") _____ , scopero ("labor strike") _____ , anno ("they have") _____ , filio ("son") _____ , songo ("dream") _____ , palla ("shovel") _____ , sono ("sleep") _____ , fato ("fact") _____ , carro ("dear") _____ .

> Some of the words in the following sentences need accent marks. Add them where appropriate.

4. Oggi e lunedi, non venerdi.
5. Che ora e? E l'una e dieci.
6. Non prendo mai il caffe, perche preferisco il te.

> The following sentences are written without capital letters. Capitalize the appropriate words according to Italian spelling conventions.

7. a primavera fa sempre fresco in italia; ma verso luglio comincia a fare più caldo. _____

8. mercoledì ho conosciuto una persona che veniva dalla spagna, ma che non parlava lo spagnolo. _____

9. la dottoressa martini è italiana, e parla molto bene l'inglese. _____

10. questo sabato vengo anche io alla festa di san pietro. _ _____

2. SUMMARIES OF WORD ORDER IN AN ITALIAN SENTENCE

> Rearrange each set of words below to form complete sentences.

11. studiano/quegli/troppo/studenti
    _____

12. troppa/Giovanni/macchina/di/la/consuma/benzina
    _____

13. dice/l'/importante/lingua/una/è/che/professoressa/la/ italiano
    _____

> Here are four object noun phrases:
>
> | l'autobus | | la radio | | ai suoi studenti | | il pianoforte |
>
> Put them into the blanks. They must, of course, fit "grammatically," completing the thought of each sentence.

14. Ieri sera, la professoressa Martini ha telefonato _____.
15. Ogni sera, Tina ascolta _____.
16. Domani aspetterò _____ davanti a ("in front of") casa tua.
17. Mia sorella suona _____ molto bene.

Answer the following two questions in the negative.

---

18. Studia l'italiano, tuo fratello?
    No, mio _____

19. Mangi il pane, tu?
    No, io _____

Match each one-word (abbreviated) answer to its
question.

---

20. **Answers**

    Sì, è vero.
    Maria.
    Bene.
    Al cinema.
    Ieri.

    Questions

    Chi aspetta l'autobus?
    Quando sono andati al
    cinema?
    Dove sono andati i tuoi
    amici?
    È italiano quell'uomo,
    vero?
    Come va, signora?

To the left you will find four main clauses in no particular order. To the right you will find four relative/tem-
poral clauses, also in no particular order. Combine
them to make four complex sentences.

---

21. *Main Clauses*

    | Quella ragazza è mia sorella |
    | È arrivato il pro-fessore |
    | Tu dormivi |
    | È necessario |

    Relative/Temporal Clauses

    | che tu dica la verità |
    | mentre io guardavo la TV |
    | appena sei andata via |
    | che legge il giornale |

    Quella ragazza _____4_____ è mia sorella.
    È arrivato il professore, _____3_____.
    Tu dormivi, _____2_____.
    È necessario _____1_____.

The following five sentences make up a story, but they
are not in order. Put them in their logical order so as to
tell the story correctly.

---

22. Durante il film hanno comprato il caffè e diverse paste.
    (*durante*/"during," *diverse*/"different," *paste*/"pastries")

1 Giovanni e Maria sono amici.
3 Hanno visto un "western" con Clint Eastwood.
5 Appena è finito il film, sono andati a prendere un gelato.
2 Ieri sono andati al cinema insieme.

_____ .
_____ .
_____ .
_____ .
_____ .

3. NOUNS

> In the following sentences, the endings of all the nouns have been removed. Can you replace them? The nouns are all singular.

23. In quella citt*à*____ c'è tanta gent*e*___ .
24. Carl*o*____ , il ragazz*o*____ che abita qui vicino, oggi non va a scuol*a*____ .
25. Il padr*e*____ e la madr*e*____ di Carl*a*____ , la ragazz*a*____ ("girlfriend") di mio fratell*o*____ , abitano in Itali*a*____ .
26. La per*a*____ viene dal per*o*____ , la mel*a*____ dal mel*o*____ , e la pesc*a*____ dal pesc*o*____ .

> Give the equivalent feminine nouns for each of the following masculine nouns.

EXAMPLE: *ragazzo ragazza*

27. zio _____ , figlio _____ , cantante _____ , infermiere _____ , cameriere _____ , pittore _____ , attore _____ , dottore _____ , avvocato _____ .

> In the following word-search puzzle there are four nouns ending in -ista. Can you find them?

28.

d	e	n	t	i	s	t	a	f	i	s	t
s	d	f	t	u	i	s	t	a	i	s	t
s	t	a	v	i	r	s	y	t	s	t	a
p	i	v	i	o	l	i	n	i	s	t	a
i	o	l	o	i	s	t	s	i	s	t	a
s	u	i	l	i	s	t	a	t	i	s	t
i	s	p	i	a	n	i	s	t	a	i	s

The answers to the following crossword puzzle are either: (1) nouns ending in an accented vowel; (2) borrowed nouns; (3) nouns ending in -ema/-amma; (4) nouns ending in -si.

29.

Across
3. crisis
4. program
5. car horn
7. tea

Down
1. thesis
2. diagram
6. sport

Put the following nouns in the plural.

EXAMPLE: *ragazzo/ragazzi*

30. giorno _____ , aeroporto _____ , cameriere _____ , notte _____ , mela _____ , avvocatessa _____ , problema _____ , programma _____ , citt _____ , computer _____ , ipotesi _____

Now put the following in the plural.

31. il tedesco, i tedes _____
la tedesca, le tedes _____
l'amico, gli ami _____
l'amica, le ami _____
il medico, i medi _____
l'albergo, gli alber _____
lo psicologo, gli psicolo _____
la psicologa, le psicolo _____
il dialogo, i dialo _____
la paga, le pa _____
la farmacia, le farmac _____
l'orologio, gli orolo _____
l'arancia, le aran _____

Try one more pluralization exercise!

32. il figlio, i _____
    la figlia, le _____
    il labbro, le _____
    il miglio, le _____
    il cinema, i _____
    l'uomo, gli _____
    la mano, le _____

Add the name "Rossi" to each of the following titles, making any appropriate changes if necessary.

EXAMPLE: *il professore*/il professor Rossi

33. il signore _____
    la signora _____
    il dottore _____
    la dottoressa _____
    l'avvocato _____

The following scrambled words are compound nouns. Unscramble them.

34. tenegslava _____
    etiviccaca _____
    rrofeiav _____
    aaoecssfrt _____
    arocbanelo _____

4.
ARTICLES

Supply the correct definite article for the following singular nouns (or adjectives).

EXAMPLE: _____ *ragazzo*/il ragazzo

35. *la* casa, *l'* acqua, *il* vino, *l'* indirizzo, *il* piatto, *la* frutta, *la* matita, *il* prezzo, *la* scuola, *la* scena, *lo* specchio, *lo* sbaglio, *il* sogno, *lo* zingaro, *lo* zio, *lo* studente, *l'* altro zio, *il* nuovo studente, *l'* altra ragazza, *lo* psicologo, *lo* gnocco

> Now supply the definite article for the following plural nouns (or adjectives).

EXAMPLE: _____ ragazzi/*i ragazzi*

36. *le* case, *le* amiche, *i* vini, *gli* indirizzi, *i* piatti, *le* frutte, *le* matite, *i* prezzi, *le* scuole, *gli* zingari, *le* scene, *gli* specchi, *gli* sbagli, *i* sogni, *gli* zii, *gli* studenti, *gli* altri zii, *i* nuovi studenti, *le* altre ragazze, *gli* psicologi, *gli* gnocchi

> Supply the indefinite article for the following nouns (or adjectives).

EXAMPLE: _____ ragazzo/*un ragazzo*

37. *un* amico, *un'* amica, *un* padre, *una* madre, *un* italiano, *un'* italiana, *un* orologio, *un'* entrata, *una* sorella, *uno* zero, *uno* zio, *uno* sbaglio, *un* altro studente, *uno* gnocco, *una* buon' amica, *uno* psicologo, *un* bravo psicologo, *una* stanza

> Supply the correct form of the demonstrative meaning "this" for the following nouns (or adjectives).

EXAMPLE: _____ amico *quest' amico*

38. *questo* giorno, *questa* valigia, *questo* nome, *questo* giornale, *questo* zio, *questa* zia, *questo* studente, *questa* studentessa, *quell'* arancio, *quest'* arancia, *questo* psicologo, *questo* infermiere, *questa* infermiera, *questo* altro zio, *questo* bravo studente

> Write the correct form of the demonstrative meaning "these" for the following nouns (or adjectives).

EXAMPLE: _____ amici *questi amici*

39. *questi* giorni, *queste* valige, *questi* nomi, *questi* giornali, *questi* zii, *queste* zie, *questi* studenti, *queste* studentesse, *questi* aranci, *queste* arance, *questi* psicologi, *questi* infermieri, *queste* infermiere, *questi* altri zii, *questi* bravi studenti

> Now write the correct form of the demonstrative meaning "that" for the following nouns (or adjectives).

EXAMPLE: _____ amico *quell'amico*

40. _____ giorno, _____ valigia, _____ nome, _____ giornale, _____ zio, _____ zia, _____ studente, _____ studentessa, _____ arancio, _____ arancia, _____ psicologo, _____ infermiere, _____ infermiera, _____ altro zio, _____ bravo studente

> Now write the correct form of the demonstrative meaning "those" for the following nouns (or adjectives).

EXAMPLE: _____ amici *quegli amici*

41. _____ giorni, _____ valige, _____ nomi, _____ giornali, _ zii, _____ zie, _____ studenti, _____ studentesse, _____ aranci, _____ arance, _____ psicologi, _____ infermieri, _____ infermiere, _____ altri zii, _____ bravi studenti

> Put the following noun phrases in the plural.

EXAMPLE: *quel ragazzo quei ragazzi*

42. la dentista _____, il farmacista _____, lo sport _____, l'entrata _____, il problema _____, l'avvocato _____, questo turista _____, questo medico _____, quest'amica _____, questa farmacia _____, quel figlio _____ , quel bacio_____ , quello zio _____, quello specchio _____, quell'orologio _____ , quell'uscita _____, quella radio _____

> Put the correct form of the definite article, if necessary, in the blanks.

43. _____ pane è un cibo.
44. _____ americani sono simpatici.
45. _____ Roma è la capitale d'Italia.
46. _____ padre e _____ madre di Claudia abitano a Parigi.
47. _____ Italia è bella.
48. Mi fa male _____ dito.
49. _____ signora Binni è molto simpatica.
50. "Buon giorno, _____ signora Binni. Come va?"

5.
PARTITIVES

> Put the following noun phrases into the plural using *di* + the definite article.

EXAMPLE: *un libro dei libri*

51. una forchetta _____ , un bicchiere _____ , uno sbaglio _____ , uno gnocco _____ , un orologio _____ , un telegramma _____ , un'avvocatessa _____ , un'automobile _____ , una sedia _____

> Now put the same nouns into the plural using *alcuni/ alcune*.

52. una forchetta _____ , un bicchiere _____ , uno sbaglio _____ , uno gnocco _____ , un orologio _____ , un telegramma _____ , un'avvocatessa _____ , un'automobile _____ , una sedia _____

> Change each partitive expression to the type with *qualche*, making all necessary changes.

EXAMPLE: *dei libri qualche libro*

53. dei ragazzi _____ , alcune studentesse _____ , delle uscite _____ , dei violinisti _____ , delle violiniste _____ , alcuni problemi _____ , alcuni uomini _____ , delle mani _____

> Rewrite each sentence, replacing the partitive expression with *qualche*, making all necessary changes.

EXAMPLE: *Alcuni studenti non studiano. Qualche studente non studia.*

54. Alcuni italiani sono simpatici. _____
55. Alcune amiche di Paola abitano in Italia. _____
_____

56. Alcuni amici di Claudio parlano il francese. _____
_____

> Rewrite the following sentences in the negative by using the *non . . . nessuno* form of the partitive. Don't forget to make all necessary changes.

EXAMPLE: *Claudia compra delle penne. Claudia non compra nessuna penna.*

57. Voglio delle caramelle. _____

_____

58. Conosco alcuni psicologi. _____

_____

59. Ho fatto degli sbagli. _____

> Give an equivalent partitive expression.

EXAMPLE: *Mangio della carne. Mangio un po' di carne.*

60. Preferisco del pane. _____
61. Giovanni mangia un po' d'insalata. _____
62. Vogliamo un po' di acqua. _____
63. Lui vuole della carne ed io voglio un po' di caffè. _____

6.
ADJECTIVES

> The adjectives *nero* (black), *verde* (green), *azzurro* (blue), *giallo* (yellow), *rosso* (red), *bianco* (white), *marrone* (brown) (invariable) are used in the following descriptive story, but their endings are missing. Supply them.

64. Maria ha un bel vestito azzurr _____ . Ieri è andata ad un negozio di abbigliamento ("clothing store") per fare alcune spese. Ha comprato un paio di scarpe ner _____, una camicetta ("blouse") verd _____ , e una sciarpa ("scarf") giall _____ . Poi, ha deciso di comprare i guanti marron _____ , un paio di pantaloni ("pants") bianch _____ , e due maglie ross _____ per suo marito. Per sua figlia ha poi comprato una maglia e una borsa verd _____ , e un cappotto e un impermeabile azzurr _____ .

> The following adjectives are already in their correct form, but now you must put them before or after the noun they modify, as the case may be.

65. (quanti) _____ libri _____ hai comprato ieri?
66. (elegante) Quello è veramente un _____ vestito _____ .
67. (quale) _____ programma _____ preferisci alla TV?
68. (molto vecchia) La conosco da tanti anni! È una _____ amica ("acquaintance") _____ .

Put the adjective *buono* in front of the noun, making all necessary changes.

EXAMPLE: *Lei è un'amica buona. Lei è una buon'amica.*

69. Quello è un libro buono. _____
70. Quella è una rivista buona. _____
71. Ho bisogno di un'auto buona. _____

Now do the same thing with the adjective *bello*.

EXAMPLE: *Sono dei libri belli. Sono dei bei libri.*

72. Mario ha comprato degli orologi belli. _____
73. Maria è veramente una donna bella. _____
74. Mia sorella vuole un'auto bella. _____
75. Giovanni ha delle amiche belle. _____

Put the proper form of *santo* in front of the following saints' names.

EXAMPLE: _____ *Anna Sant'Anna*

76. _____ Maria, _____ Stefano, _____ Agostino, _____ Paolo, _____ Marco, _____ Agnese

Using an interrogative adjective, formulate the appropriate question for each of the following.

EXAMPLE: *Ho comprato due libri./Quanti libri hai comprato?*

77. Preferisco quella macchina. _____ ?
78. È un libro interessante. _____ ?
79. Ho mangiato tre panini ("sandwiches"). _____ ?

Provide the missing parts of the following possessive adjectives.

EXAMPLE: _____ *su* _____ *penna la sua penna*

80. _____ mi _____ libri, _____ mi _____ giacca, _____ mi _____ amiche, _____ mi _____ quaderno, _____ tu _____ vestito, _____ tu _____ scarpe, _____ tu _____ casa, _____ tu _____ impermeabili, _____ su _____ libro, _____ su _____ libri, _____ su _____ amica, _____ su _____ amiche, _____ nostr _____ dottore, _____ nostr _____ professori, _____ nostr _____ professoressa, _____ nostr _____

professoresse, _____ vostr _____ riviste, _____ vostr
_____ amica, _____ vostr _____ sbaglio _____ vostr _____
sbagli, _____ lor _____ problema, _____ _____ lor
_____problemi, _____ lor _____ casa, _____ lor _____
case

Make the following noun phrases singular. But be careful! There are many "traps" in this exercise.

EXAMPLE: *i nostri zii* <u>*nostro zio*</u>

81. i tuoi cugini _____ , le nostre zie _____ , le vostre cugine
_____ , i loro fratelli _____ , le loro sorelle _____ , i suoi
zii italiani _____ , le sue cugine americane _____ ,
i vostri papà _____

Can you figure out the following family relationships?

EXAMPLE: *È la madre di mio padre. È* <u>*mia nonna.*</u>

82. È il figlio di tuo zio. È _____
È la sorella di nostra madre. È _____
È il fratello di suo padre. È _____
È il marito (husband) della loro madre. È _____

Here is a logic puzzle for you.

---

83. Un bambino risponde al telefono. "Pronto. Chi parla?"
La voce (voice) di un uomo dice: "La madre di tua
madre è mia suocera (mother-in-law)." Chi è l'uomo?

The following indefinite adjectives are missing from the passage.
     assai, altre, molti, troppa, stesse, tutti
Put them in their appropriate slots.

---

84. _____ turisti vanno in Italia. Purtroppo, hanno bisogno
di _____ denaro (money) per andare a vedere _____ i
bei posti (places) di questo magnifico paese (country).
Dappertutto (everywhere) c'è _____ gente. Tutti hanno
le _____ idee. Vogliono vedere Roma, Venezia, Firenze,
e Napoli. Ma ci sono tante _____ belle città!

> Make an appropriate comparison.

EXAMPLE: *Maria è intelligente. Giovanni è meno intelligente. Giovanni è meno intelligente di Maria.* OR *Maria è più intelligente di Giovanni.*

85. Mio padre è elegante. Tuo padre è altrettanto elegante (as elegant) _____

    _____

86. Gino è simpatico. Mario è più simpatico. _____

    _____

87. Gino è simpatico, ma è più intelligente. _____

    _____

7. PRONOUNS

> Supply the corresponding pronoun for each noun phrase.

EXAMPLE: *Quel ragazzo è italiano. Quello è italiano.*

88. Questo negozio è caro. _____ è caro.
    Queste ragazze sono americane. _____ sono americane.
    Quest'orologio è nuovo. _____ è nuovo.
    Quest'auto è bella. _____ è bella.
    Quei francobolli ("stamps") sono belli. _____ sono belli.
    Quello zio abita in Italia. _____ abita in Italia.
    Quegli amici sono bravi. _____ sono bravi.
    Quelle forchette sono sporche. _____ sono sporche.
    Quel vino è molto buono. _____ è molto buono.

> Do the same thing for the following.

EXAMPLE: *La sua macchina è bella. La sua è bella.*

89. Dove sono i tuoi guanti? Dove sono _____ ?
    Il loro impermeabile è verde. _____ è verde.
    Chi ha le mie scarpe? Chi ha _____ ?
    Nostra sorella abita in Italia. _____ abita in Italia.
    Suo zio è simpatico. _____ è simpatico.

> Using interrogative pronouns, formulate the appropriate question for each of the following.

EXAMPLE: *Leggo un libro. Che cosa leggi?*

90. Giovanni abita a Roma. _____ ?
91. Questo portafoglio è di Bruno. _____ ?

92. Mi chiamo Giuseppe Perri. _____ ?
93. Abito in via Dante, 24. _____ ?
94. Sono andato in Italia l'anno scorso. _____ ?
95. Mangio i dolci perché mi piacciono. _____ ?

Supply the appropriate subject personal pronouns.
These are needed in the passage in order to distinguish all the different persons involved.

---

96. L'altro giorno, _____ sono andato al cinema con mia
   sorella, e _____ ha portato con sé un libro da leggere!
   Quando _____ due siamo arrivati, abbiamo visto due
   amici nostri. Anche _____ erano venuti al cinema.
   "Gianni, Maria, siete proprio _____?" ha chiesto mia
   sorella. "Certo che siamo _____!" ha risposto Maria.
   "_____ sono qui per Gianni, e _____?" Maria ha chiesto
   a mia sorella. "Purtroppo anche _____ sono qui per mio
   fratello!" ha risposto mia sorella.

Replace each of the object pronouns with equivalent
ones, rewriting each sentence and making all necessary changes.

EXAMPLE: *Lui dà la penna a me. Lui mi dà la penna.*

97. Giovanni telefonerà a loro domani. _____
98. Penso spesso a te. _____
99. Maria ha chiamato me. _____
100. Chiamerò lui domani. _____
101. Tu telefonerai a lui. _____
102. Maria chiamerà lei. _____
103. E poi telefonerà a lei. _____
104. Maria ha visto noi ieri. _____
105. Il professore parlerà a voi. _____

Now replace each object noun phrase with *lo, la, li, le,*
or *gli* as the case may be. Rewrite each sentence,
making all necessary changes.

EXAMPLE: *Giovanni ha comprato quelle penne. Giovanni le ha*
                                                    comprate.

106. Ha già dato *la penna* a quel ragazzo. _____
    Ha già dato la penna *a quella ragazza.* _____
    Ieri abbiamo mangiato *il pollo.* _____
    Ieri abbiamo telefonato *a quel ragazzo.* _____

Giovanni mi ha dato *le sue chiavi*. _____
Mio padre gli ha mandato *i suoi libri*. _____
Il commesso ci ha detto *la verità*. _____
No, non ho dato le mie scarpe *a tua sorella*. _____
Sì, ha mandato *quella lettera al tuo amico*. _____

_____

Use object pronouns to answer each question.

EXAMPLE: *Hai dato la penna a Maria? Sì gliel'ho data.*

107. Mi hai chiamato ieri? Sì, _____
108. Ti hanno telefonato? No, _____
109. Hai ricevuto la lettera? Sì, _____
110. Mi darai il tuo indirizzo? No, _____
111. Ci scriverai una lettera? Sì, _____

Rearrange each set of words below to form complete sentences.

112. scritte / gliele / già / ho _____
113. le / mando / ve / domani _____
114. te / dati / li / ieri / ho _____

The relative pronouns are missing from the following passage. Can you supply them?

115. Il vestito _____ ho comprato ieri costa poco. Il commesso, dal _____ l'ho comprato, era molto simpatico. Mi ha spiegato ("explained") _____ il verde era il colore d'ultimo grido ("in the latest fashion"). "Questo vestito è per mia figlia, a _____ lo darò domani per il suo compleanno ("birthday"). _____ mi piace in modo particolare è la sua lunghezza ("length")."

The pronouns *ne, ci* (there), and *si* (one) (impersonal form) are missing from the following sentences. Put them in the appropriate slot.

116. Non _____ dicono queste cose!
117. Quanta _____ hai mangiata?
118. _____ andremo fra due mesi.
119. Non _____ è mai contenti!
120. _____ sono andati, e poi _____ sono tornati.

**8.
VERBS**

Each one of the following sentences requires that the verb (given to you in its infinitive form) be put into one of the seven indicative tenses. There is enough information in each sentence for you to figure out which tense is appropriate.

EXAMPLE: *Fra una settimana, noi* <u>andare</u> *in Italia.* Ans:
andremo

121. Tu _____ (*uscire*) già, quando sono arrivato io.
Che cosa _____ (*comprare*) tu ieri?
Quando ero bambino, i miei genitori _____ (*andare*) spesso in Italia per riposarsi ("to relax").
Dopo che gli ospiti (guests) _____ (*mangiare*) gli spaghetti, allora servirò la carne.
Quanto costa la tua borsa? Non sono sicura. _____ (*costare*) 100.000 lire.
Appena finimmo di lavorare, noi _____ (*cominciare*) a giocare a tennis.
Lo _____ (*pagare*) tu il conto, o lo pago io?

The following exercise is almost the same. This time, however, you must choose the correct verb and then put it in the appropriate indicative tense.

VERBS: cominciare, mangiare, finire, capire, arrivare,
scrivere, mettere

122. Anche tu _____ l'insalata? Io l'ho già mangiata. Io _____ a leggere, appena sarà finito quel programma alla TV.
I nostri amici _____ dall'Italia pochi minuti fa.
Quando ha finito? Non sono sicuro. _____ alcune ore fa.
Giovanni non _____ la domanda, perché non la sentì (because he didn't hear it).
Mentre lei _____ una lettera, io dormivo.
Giovanni, dove _____ quella forchetta?

Here's an easy one. Match up the pronouns and verbs.

123. Pronouns	Verbs
io	finiscono la lezione
tu	è uscita
lui	paghiamo il conto
lei	parlate troppo
noi	non aspetto
voi	è uscito
loro	capisci

> Choose the appropriate imperative form.

124. Signor Santini, { lo prenda! ☐ / prendilo! ☐ }

Marco, { la scriva! ☐ / scrivila! ☐ }

Signorina, { me li dia! ☐ / dammeli! ☐ }

Gino, { non parli! ☐ / non parlare! ☐ }

Ragazzi, { ci andate! ☐ / andateci! ☐ }

> Now it's time for the conditional tenses. Put each verb in the present or past conditional, as the case may be.

EXAMPLE: *Anche noi ci _saremmo andati_ (andare), ma non avevamo tempo.*

125. (Io) ti _____ (*scrivere*) volentieri, ma non ho tempo.
(Io) ti _____ (*scrivere*) volentieri, ma non ho avuto tempo.
Giovanni _____ (*mangiare*) tutto, ma purtroppo non aveva tempo.
Anche in questo momento ha appetito, e lui _____ (*mangiare*) tutto.

> Here's a simple exercise. Choose one of the two verbs provided. One is in the indicative and the other in the subjunctive, but only one of the two fits in each sentence.

126. Maria dice che il professore { arriverà ☐ / arrivi ☐ } tra due minuti.

Maria spera che il professore { finisce ☐ / finisca ☐ } presto.

Sebbene { ha piovuto ☐ / abbia piovuto ☐ } ieri, sono uscita lo stesso.

Se { lavorerai ☐ / lavorassi ☐ } fino a tardi, non potremo andare al cinema.

Se quella donna { potrà ☐ / potesse ☐ } , ti telefonerebbe.

Era la persona più $\begin{cases} \text{avevamo conosciuto} & \square \text{ in} \\ \text{avessimo conosciuto} & \square \text{ Italia.} \end{cases}$
simpatica che noi

Supply the missing parts of the following reflexive verbs.

---

127. Ieri ci _____ divertiti molto in centro (downtown).
     A che ora _____ alzi tu ogni mattina?
     La dottoressa Visconti non _____ ricorda il nostro indirizzo.
     Anche voi ragazze, vi siete divertit _____ , no?
     No, non me la sono lavat _____ !
     Giovanni, alza _____ subito!
     Signora, _____ metta questo cappotto!

Here is Giovanni's love letter to Elena. Since Giovannia does not like to study his verbs, he has left out their endings, or some other parts. Can you complete the verbs?

---

128. Mia cara Elena,

non ti scriv _____ da tanto tempo, perché _____ stato molto occupato ("busy"). Ieri, benché la giornata _____ stata terribile, sono uscito a compr _____ un regalo. Mentre _____ guardando le vetrine ("store windows"), è venut _____ un uomo vicino a me. Vol _____ parlare, ma io non av _____ tempo. Ma lui _____ cominciato a parlare lo stesso. Mi _____ parlato per un'ora. Io speravo che and _____ via. Finalmente, dopo aver parl _____ a lungo (for a long time), decise di and _____ via.

Quando sar _____ insieme ti dar _____ il regalo. Ti am _____ .

Tuo,

Giovannaccio!

Here's a chance for you to review those irregular verbs, which you can find in the "Verb Charts" section of this book. Each of the following verbs has an irregular past participle hidden in the word-search puzzle. Can you find them?

---

bere, chiedere, chiudere, dire, essere, fare, leggere, mettere, nascere, prendere, scegliere, scrivere

129.

t	u	i	u	h	n	b	e	v	u	t	o	c	i	o
d	c	l	e	t	t	o	m	e	s	s	o	h	s	n
e	p	h	p	r	e	s	o	d	e	c	t	i	u	a
t	r	r	i	f	t	u	t	i	o	r	t	e	o	t
t	e	i	h	u	u	i	t	b	m	i	n	s	p	o
o	s	g	h	t	s	o	a	h	u	t	k	t	t	o
e	s	t	a	t	o	o	f	o	o	t	o	o	t	o
c	h	i	e	d	s	c	e	l	t	o	d	i	t	t

Change the following sentences into their passive form.

130. Giovanni ha mangiato la torta.
I turisti compreranno molti regali.
Tutti leggono quel libro.
Credo che Sofia Loren abbia interpretato (interpreted) quel film.

9.
ADVERBS

Change the following adjectives into adverbs of manner.

EXAMPLE: *lento lentamente*

131. raro _____ , certo _____ , preciso _____ , vero _____ , nuovo _____

Now do the same with these.

EXAMPLE: *facile facilmente*

132. elegante _____ , felice _____ , regolare _____ , difficile _____ , popolare _____ , benevolo _____ , leggero _____

Put each of the following adverbs in the blanks according to the context.

ancora, invece, già, poi, quasi, spesso

133. Sono _____ partiti per l'Italia.
134. So che tu preferisci quella camicia, ma io, _____ , preferisco questa.
135. Non è _____ l'ora di andare a casa.
136. Prima devo studiare, e _____ posso guardare la TV.
137. Noi andiamo _____ al cinema. Infatti, ci andiamo _____ ogni settimana.

> *Molto* is both an adverb and an adjective. Supply the appropriate form of this word.

138. Ieri avevo _____ fame. Allora ho mangiato _____ . Gli spaghetti erano _____ buoni. Anche la carne era _____ _____ buona. A tavola c'erano _____ persone. Tutti hanno mangiato _____ verdure e _____ carne.

> Now add either *migliore* or *meglio*.

139. Quello è un vino _____ .
140. Il mio orologio funziona _____ del tuo.
141. È la _____ cosa che tu abbia potuto fare.
142. Oggi sto _____ (I feel better) di ieri.

10. PREPOSI-TIONS

> Put *a, di, da, su,* or *in* in the appropriate blanks according to the meaning. Don't forget contractions!

EXAMPLE: Questo è il libro di + il = del professore
(*di + il = del*)   + il = _____

143. Ho messo la chiave _____ + *il* cassetto. = _____ cassetto.
Il libro è _____ + *il* = _____ tavolo.
Ieri ho scritto _____ + *gli* = _____ zii di Pina.
È l'indirizzo _____ + *lo* = _____ studente.
Sono venuto _____ + *l'* = _____ Italia una settimana fa.
C'è una caramella _____ + *la* = _____ scatola.

> Put the following sentences in the plural.

144. È il libro dell'amico di Carla. _____
145. Ieri sono andata al negozio di abbigliamento. _____
_____
146. È nello zaino (knapsack). _____
147. Dall'uscita potrai vedere la macchina. _____
_____
148. Ho dato la tua matita alla ragazza. _____

> Put each of the following prepositions in the blanks according to the context.

a, in, da, tra, per

149. Abito in questa città _____ tre anni. Spero, _____ due anni, di andare _____ Francia _____ studiare il francese. Vorrei andare _____ Parigi (Paris).

11. NEGATIVES AND OTHER GRAMMAT- ICAL POINTS

> The negatives in the following sentences are scrambled up. Can you unscramble them?

150. I miei parenti non scrivono "ami" _____ .
     Non conosciamo "esnsnou" _____ in quella città.
     Alla nostra festa non è venuto "eannhce" _____ Gino.
     Non capisco "én" _____ i pronomi "én" _____ i verbi.
     Ti prometto (I promise you) che non lo faccio
     "ipù" _____ .
     Sono andato in quel negozio, ma non ho comprato
     "ieennt" _____ .
     Quello che tu dici non è "icma" _____ vero.

> Put è, *sono, c'è, ci sono,* or *ecco* in the blanks, as the case may be.

151. Dov'è il mio cappotto? _____ il tuo cappotto!
152. L'ho messo nel cassetto, ma ora non _____ più.
153. Qual _____ il tuo programma preferito?
154. Dove _____ i tuoi libri? In questa stanza non _____ .

> Rearrange each set of words below to form a complete sentence. Here is a clue to help you: each sentence contains the "causative" construction.

155. cartolina / zii / fatto / scrivere / ha / agli / madre / la / una

     _____

     _____

156. comprare / gliela / farò _____
157. suo / a / fratello / Maria / lavare / non / fatto / ha / piatti / i _____

     _____

12. THE VERB *PIACERE*

> Giovanni has been studying Italian and understands it well. However, he is a little shy about speaking it. In the following dialogue with Maria — who speaks and understands English — Giovanni uses only English because he is afraid to use the verb "piacere." Can you help him out by translating what he says into Italian?

   Maria: Ciao, Giovanni. Vedo che vai a lezione (to class). Ti piace il corso d'italiano?

158. *Giovanni*: Yes, I like it very much. _____.
     Maria: Ti piace la professoressa?

159. *Giovanni*: Yes, I like her and she likes me. _____
_____ .

Maria: E gli altri studenti?

160. *Giovanni*: I like them, but they do not like me. _____
_____ .

Maria: E io so perché. Tu sei antipatico! Ti è piaciuta la lezione di ieri?

161. *Giovanni*: No, I didn't like it, and the others didn't like it.
_____ .

Maria: E io ti piaccio?

162. *Giovanni*: Yes, I like you. Do you like me? Do we like each other, really? _____ .
Maria: Certamente. Andiamo. La lezione sta per cominciare.

Put either *piace* or *piacciono* in the blanks, as the case may be.

---

163. Sì, mi _____ la tua cravatta, ma non mi _____ i tuoi pantaloni.
164. Ci _____ i tortellini, ma purtroppo non ci _____ il sugo ("sauce").
165. Ti _____ la minestra? A me non _____ , ma mi _____ i ravioli.
166. A lui _____ l'italiano, a me _____ gli sport, a te _____ il cinema, a tutti noi non _____ le barzellette ("jokes").

13. IDIOMATIC EXPRES- SIONS

Give the Italian of the English words in italics.

---

167. Giovanni ed io *are hungry and thirsty* _____.
168. D'estate loro *are always hot* _____ , ma d'inverno *they are always cold* _____.
169. Signora, Lei *are right* _____ ; io, invece, *am wrong* __.
170. Giovanni, non devi *be ashamed* _____ , e non devi *be afraid*. Vedrai che tutto andrà bene.
171. *I feel like* _____ di andare ad un ristorante stasera.
172. We *need* _____ due cose quando andremo in centro.

Insert *fare, dare,* or *stare* in the right tense and mood, as the case may be.

Commesso: Buongiorno, signora. Desidera?

173. *Signora*: Buongiorno, voglio _____ il biglietto per il treno che parte per Roma tra un'ora.

174. *Commesso*: Va bene. Ma _____ retta a ma! C'è un treno che _____ per partire in questo momento.

175. *Signora*: Per me va bene anche quello. _____ pure il biglietto. Le posso _____ una domanda? Lei si _____ la barba alla mattina?

176. *Commesso*: Lei è impertinente! Farmi la barba, non _ per me. Perché mi _____ questa domanda? Le _____ fastidio.
    Signora: No, anzi, a me piacciono gli uomini con la barba!

The following crossword puzzle contains only parts of the expressions defined in the clues. Can you complete it?

177.

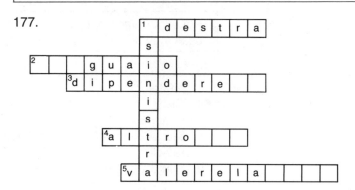

Across
1. to the right
2. What a mess
3. to depend on
4. I'll say!
5. to be worthwhile

Down
1. to the left

14. NUMBERS

Write out each number in words.

178. 7 _____ , 9 _____ , 11 _____ , 21 _____ , 42 _____ , 58 _____ , 88 _____ , 123 _____ , 987 _____ , 1.345 _____ , 76.980 _____ , 888.888 _____ , 2.345.678 _____ .

Now do the same for the following ordinal numbers.

---

179. 4th _____ ragazza, 16th _____ lezioni, 23rd _____ sbaglio, 248th _____ giorno, 4,578th _____ pagina

> Now write the following fractions in words.

180. ⅔ _____ , ¹⁄₂₈ _____ , ¾ _____ , ¹⁵⁄₁₆ _____ , ³⁴⁄₈₉ _____

> Are you a math whiz? Try the following.

181. Maria ha due anni più di Gina. Gina ha tre anni meno di Claudia, la quale ha otto anni. Quanti anni ha Maria?

Marco e Gino insieme hanno ventidue anni. Gino ha due anni più di Marco. Quanti anni ha ogni ragazzo?

Giovanni è più alto di Stefano. Stefano è meno alto di Claudio. Chi è il più basso?

15.
TELLING TIME

> Write out the time indicated on each watch. Use the twenty-four-hour-clock, or official time.

182. Che ora è?

16.
DAYS, MONTHS, SEASONS, DATES, AND THE WEATHER

Can you find the days of the week hidden in the word-search puzzle?

183.

b	ì	s	t	g	i	o	v	e	d	ì
q	r	y	p	m	e	l	e	w	c	k
a	x	v	o	n	i	z	n	u	d	y
p	n	m	a	b	o	v	e	n	l	r
t	h	a	s	o	l	k	r	t	l	o
m	e	r	c	o	l	e	d	ì	s	a
x	c	t	e	j	u	g	ì	h	a	r
v	w	e	t	o	n	i	k	a	b	l
j	u	d	o	m	e	n	i	c	a	x
p	h	ì	r	e	d	a	s	o	t	g
z	k	a	y	n	ì	n	o	b	o	r

Here are the months of the year all scrambled up. Can you unscramble them?

184. berttoo _____
 uoilgl _____
 toogsa _____
 erbemidc _____
 ttseeermb _____
 erbmevno _____
 oiaegnn _____
 uiggon _____
 oaibbref _____
 ggmmioa _____
 leirpa _____
 ozrma _____

Fill in the blanks with the appropriate words.

185. La _____ è la prima stagione dell'anno.
 Durante l' _____ andiamo sempre a sciare ("to ski").
 La settimana _____ sono andato in Italia.
 Il mese _____ andremo a Roma.
 Tre giorni _____ ho incontrato ("I met") Claudia.
 Ciao. _____ domani!

Maria found Giovanni's diary, which she is just dying to read. Everything is written in Italian except the dates. Can you translate them for her?

186. Monday, May 12: "Amo Maria!" _____
 Tuesday, January 25: "Amo ancora Maria!" _____

Wednesday, February 1: "Non amo più Maria!" _____
Saturday, December 3: "Amo Claudia!" _____

> Match each of the following expressions with the drawings.

EXPRESSIONS: tuona e lampeggia, tira vento, fa molto caldo, fa freddo, fa bel tempo, piove

187.

_____   _____   _____

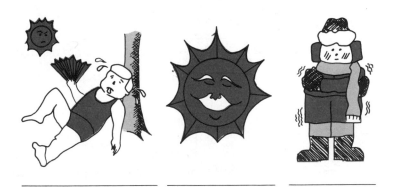

_____   _____   _____

17.
COMMON
DISCOURSE
STRATEGIES

> Fill in the missing parts of the following dialogue.

188. *il signor Marchi*: Buon giorno, signora. _____?
la signora Celli: Non _____ , grazie, e _____?
il signor Marchi: Molto bene. Dove va?
la signora Celli: Vado in biblioteca, e ho molto fretta. ArrivederLa.
il signor Marchi: B _____.

> Now do the same for the following dialogue.

189. *Lucia*: Pronto. _____ parla?
Gino: Ciao, Lucia. _____ Gino. _____ tua sorella?
Lucia: No. È uscita per fare delle spese. Hai bisogno di qualcosa?
Gino: No, grazie. Telefono più tardi. Ciao.
Lucia: A _____ .

> Here's one more for you to do!

190. *il professore*: Buona sera, signorina.
la signorina: _____ , professore.
il professore: _____ _____ chiama?
la signorina: Mi _____ Daniela Berti. Professore, permette che _____ presenti un'altra studentessa. _____ presento Dina Armando.
il professore: _____ di fare la Sua _____ .
Dina: Grazie, professore.

> Check off the appropriate expression for each of the following.

191. You're bored. You might say:
Non importa ☐
Che noia! ☐
Fa lo stesso. ☐
192. You might want to tell someone that you are sorry. You might say:
Mi dispiace. ☐
Che triste! ☐
Pazienza! ☐
193. You want to say that you do not agree. You might say:
D'accordo. ☐
Non va bene. ☐
Non sono d'accordo. ☐
194. How would you say: "How come?"
Davvero? ☐
Come? ☐
Scherzi? ☐

**18.
SYNONYMS
AND
ANTONYMS**

Can you match the synonyms in each column?

195. ora
abito
vicino
faccia
volentieri
quindi
pazzo
chiedere

domandare
matto
viso
dunque
adesso
vestito
presso
con piacere

Fill in the blanks with either *sapere* or *conoscere*, as
the case may be. Don't forget to put them in their
appropriate tense and mood.

196. Ieri (io) _____ la professoressa d'italiano.
Quando avrò studiato con lei, allora _____ bene
l'italiano.
Quando ero bambino, _____ suonare il pianoforte.
È impossibile che tu non _____ Roma.

Can you match the antonyms in each column?

197. piccolo
magro
dentro
aperto
pulito
alba
chiaro
atterraggio
presto

chiuso
tramonto
tardi
sporco
fuori
decollo
grande
scuro
grasso

**19.
COGNATES:
GOOD AND
FALSE
FRIENDS**

Supply the Italian equivalent for the following English
words.

EXAMPLE: nation *la nazione*

198. condition _____
conclusion _____
importance _____
vocabulary _____
oculist _____
geology _____
social _____
effect _____

situation _____
society _____
actor _____
violinist _____
biology _____
typical _____
perfect _____
intellect _____

Check off the correct meaning of each word.

199. *la libreria*
il negozio dove si comprano i libri ☐
il luogo dove i libri sono a disposizione del pubblico ☐

il parente
il padre o la madre ☐
lo zio, la zia, il cugino . . . ☐

la fattoria
la casa "in campagna" ☐
un luogo industriale ☐

la stampa
si mette su una busta da lettera ☐
si "legge" ☐

Translate the italicized words into Italian.

200. Domani, *I will be present* _____ alla riunione (meeting).
Ieri, quell'uomo ha avuto *an accident* _____ brutto.
Arturo Toscanini era un grande *conductor* _____.
Non mi piace *that magazine* _____.
Giovanni lavora per *a big firm* _____.

Answers

1.
ITALIAN SOUNDS AND SPELLING

1. (*see* §1.3) cane, cravatta, come, gola, grande, spaghetti, chiesa, ghiaccio
2. (*see* §1.3) ciao, giorno, cena, giro, cioccolata, gente, cinema, giacca
3. scherzo, scena, sciopero, hanno, figlio, sogno, pala, sonno, fatto, caro (*see* §1.3)
4. (*see* §1.4) Oggi è lunedì, non venerdì.
5. (*see* §1.4) Che ora è? È l'una e dieci.
6. (*see* §1.4) Non prendo mai il caffè, perché preferisco il tè.
7. (*see* §1.5) A primavera fa sempre fresco in Italia; ma verso luglio comincia a fare più caldo.
8. (*see* §1.5) Mercoledì ho conosciuto una persona che veniva dalla Spagna, ma che non parlava lo spagnolo.
9. (*see* §1.5) La dottoressa Martini è italiana, e parla molto bene l'inglese.
10. (*see* § 1.5) Questo sabato vengo anche io alla festa di San Pietro.

2.
WORD ORDER
IN AN ITALIAN
SENTENCE

11–13 (§2.1 and general knowledge of word order)
11. Quegli studenti studiano troppo.
12. La macchina di Giovanni consuma troppa benzina.
13. La professoressa dice che l'italiano è una lingua importante.
14–17 (*see* §2.2–1)
14. Ieri sera, la professoressa Martini ha telefonato ai suoi studenti.
15. Ogni sera, Tina ascolta la radio.
16. Domani aspetterò l'autobus davanti a casa tua.
17. Mia sorella suona il pianoforte molto bene.
18, 19 (*see* § 2.2–2 and §2.2–3)
18. No, mio fratello non studia l'italiano.
19. No, io non mangio il pane.
20. (*see* §2.2–3 and §2.4)
     Chi aspetta l'autobus? —Maria.
     Quando sono andati al cinema? —Ieri.
     Dove sono andati i tuoi amici? —Al cinema.
     È italiano quell'uomo, vero? —Sì, è vero.
     Come va, signora? —Bene.
21. (*see* §2.3–1 and §2.3–2)
     Quella ragazza che legge il giornale è mia sorella.
     È arrivato il professore, appena sei andata via.
     Tu dormivi, mentre io guardavo la TV.
     È necessario che tu dica la verità.
22. Giovanni e Maria sono amici. Ieri sono andati al cinema insieme. Hanno visto un "western" con Clint Eastwood. Durante il film hanno comprato il caffè e diverse paste. Appena è finito il film, sono andati a prendere un gelato.

§3.
Nouns

23–26 (*see* §3.2)
23. In quella città c'è tanta gente.
24. Carlo, il ragazzo che abita qui vicino, oggi non va a scuola.
25. Il padre e la madre di Carla, la ragazza di mio fratello, abitano in Italia.
26. La pera viene dal pero, la mela dal melo, e la pesca dal pesco.
27. (*see* §3.2–1)
     zia, figlia, cantante, infermiera, cameriera, pittrice, attrice, dottoressa, avvocatessa

28. (*see* §3.2–2)

d	e	n	t	i	s	t	a	f	i	s	t
s	d	f	t	u	i	s	t	a	i	s	t
s	t	a	v	i	r	s	y	t	s	t	a
p	i	v	i	o	l	i	n	i	s	t	a
i	o	l	o	i	s	t	s	i	s	t	a
s	u	i	l	i	s	t	a	t	i	s	t
i	s	p	i	a	n	i	s	t	a	i	s

29. (*see* §3.2–3 through §3.2–6)

30. (*see* §3.3–1 through §3.3–3)
   giorni, aeroporti, camerieri, notti, mele, avvocatesse,
   problemi, programmi, città, computer, ipotesi

31. (*see* §3.3–4)
   i tedeschi
   le tedesche
   gli amici
   le amiche
   i medici
   gli alberghi
   gli psicologi
   le psicologhe
   i dialoghi
   le paghe
   le farmacie
   gli orologi
   le arance

32. (*see* §3.3–5, §3.3–6)
    i figli
    le figlie
    le labbra
    le miglia
    i cinema
    gli uomini
    le mani

33. (*see* §3.4)
    il signor Rossi
    la signora Rossi
    il dottor Rossi
    la dottoressa Rossi
    l'avvocato Rossi

34. (*see* §3.6)
    salvagente
    cacciavite
    ferrovia
    cassaforte
    arcobaleno

4.
ARTICLES

35. (*see* §4.2–1)
    la casa, l'acqua, il vino, l'indirizzo, il piatto, la frutta, la
    matita, il prezzo, la scuola, la scena, lo specchio, lo
    sbaglio, il sogno, lo zingaro, lo zio, lo studente, l'altro
    zio, il nuovo studente, l'altra ragazza, lo psicologo, lo
    gnocco

36. (*see* §4.2–1)
    le case, le amiche, i vini, gli indirizzi, i piatti, le frutte, le
    matite, i prezzi, le scuole, le scene, gli specchi, gli
    sbagli, i sogni, gli zingari, gli zii, gli studenti, gli altri zii, i
    nuovi studenti, le altre ragazze, gli psicologi, gli gnocchi

37. (*see* §4.2–2)
    un amico, un'amica, un padre, una madre, un italiano,
    un'italiana, un orologio, un'entrata, una sorella, uno
    zero, uno zio, uno sbaglio, un altro studente, uno
    gnocco, una buon'amica, uno psicologo, un bravo
    psicologo, una stanza

38. (*see* §4.2–3)
    questo giorno, questa valigia, questo nome, questo
    giornale, questo zio, questa zia, questo studente,
    questa studentessa, questo (quest') arancio, questa
    (quest') arancia, questo psicologo, questo (quest')
    infermiere, questa (quest') infermiera, questo (quest')
    altro zio, questo bravo studente

39. (*see* §4.2–3)
    questi giorni, queste valige, questi nomi, questi giornali, questi zii, queste zie, questi studenti, queste studentesse, questi aranci, queste arance, questi psicologi, questi infermieri, queste infermiere, questi altri zii, questi bravi studenti
40. (*see* §4.2–3)
    quel giorno, quella valigia, quel nome, quel giornale, quello zio, quella zia, quello studente, quella studentessa, quell'arancio, quell'arancia, quello psicologo, quell'infermiere, quell'infermiera, quell'altro zio, quel bravo studente
41. (*see* §4.2–3)
    quei giorni, quelle valige, quei nomi, quei giornali, quegli zii, quelle zie, quegli studenti, quelle studentesse, quegli aranci, quelle arance, quegli psicologi, quegli infermieri, quelle infermiere, quegli altri zii, quei bravi studenti
42. (*review* Chapters 3 and 4)
    le dentiste, i farmacisti, gli sport, le entrate, i problemi, gli avvocati, questi turisti, questi medici, queste amiche, queste farmacie, quei figli, quei baci, quegli zii, quegli specchi, quegli orologi, quelle uscite, quelle radio
43–50 (*see* 4.3)
43. Il pane è un cibo.
44. Gli americani sono simpatici.
45. Roma è la capitale d'Italia (*no article*).
46. Il padre e la madre di Claudia abitano a Parigi.
47. L'Italia è bella.
48. Mi fa male il dito.
49. La signora Binni è molto simpatica.
50. "Buon giorno, signora Binni. Come va?" (*no article*)

5. PARTITIVES

51–59 (*see* §5.2)
51. delle forchette, dei bicchieri, degli sbagli, degli gnocchi, degli orologi, dei telegrammi, delle avvocatesse, delle automobili, delle sedie
52. alcune forchette, alcuni bicchieri, alcuni sbagli, alcuni gnocchi, alcuni orologi, alcuni telegrammi, alcune avvocatesse, alcune automobili, alcune sedie
53. qualche ragazzo, qualche studentessa, qualche uscita, qualche violinista, qualche violinista, qualche problema, qualche uomo, qualche mano
54. Qualche italiano è simpatico.
55. Qualche amica di Paola abita in Italia.

56. Qualche amico di Claudio parla il francese.
57. Non voglio nessuna caramella.
58. Non conosco nessuno psicologo.
59. Non ho fatto nessuno sbaglio.
60–63 (*see* §5.3)
60. Preferisco un po' di pane.
61. Giovanni mangia dell'insalata.
62. Vogliamo dell'acqua.
63. Lui vuole un po' di carne e io voglio del caffè.

6.
ADJECTIVES

64. (*see* §6.2)
    . . . azzurro . . . nere . . . verde . . . gialla . . . marrone
    . . . bianchi . . . rosse . . . verdi . . . azzurri
65–68 (*see* §6.3)
65. Quanti libri hai comprato ieri?
66. Quello è veramente un vestito elegante.
67. Quale programma preferisci alla TV?
68. La conosco da tanti anni! È una conoscenza molto vecchia.
69–76 (*see* §6.4–1)
69. Quello è un buon libro.
70. Quella è una buona rivista.
71. Ho bisogno di una buon'auto.
72. Mario ha comprato dei begli orologi.
73. Maria è veramente una bella donna.
74. Mia sorella vuole una bell'auto.
75. Giovanni ha delle belle amiche.
76. Santa Maria, Santo Stefano, Sant'Agostino, San Paolo, San Marco, Sant'Agnese
77–79 (*see* §6.4–2)
77. Quale macchina preferisci (preferisce, Lei)?
78. Che (libro) è?
79. Quanti panini hai mangiato?
80–83 (*see* §6.4–3)
80. i miei libri, la mia giacca, le mie amiche, il mio quaderno, il tuo vestito, le tue scarpe, la tua casa, i tuoi impermeabili, il suo libro, i suoi libri, la sua amica, le sue amiche, il nostro dottore, i nostri professori, la nostra professoressa, le nostre professoresse, le vostre riviste, la vostra amica, il vostro sbaglio, i vostri sbagli, il loro problema, i loro problemi, la loro casa, le loro case
81. tuo cugino, nostra zia, vostra cugina, il loro fratello, la loro sorella, il suo zio italiano, la sua cugina americana, il vostro papà

82. È tuo cugino.
    È nostra zia.
    È suo zio.
    È il loro padre.
83. È il padre del bambino.
84. (*see* §6.4–4)
    Molti turisti . . . assai denaro . . . tutti i bei posti . . .
    troppa gente . . .stesse idee . . . altre belle città
85–87 (*see* §6.5)
85. Tuo padre è (così) elegante come mio padre./Tuo
    padre è (tanto) elegante quanto mio padre. (Or you can
    change *tuo padre* and *mio padre* around.)
86. Mario è più simpatico di Gino./Gino è meno simpatico
    di Mario.
87. Gino è più intelligente che simpatico./Gino è meno sim-
    patico che intelligente.

7. PRONOUNS

88–95 (*see* §7.2)
88. Questo è caro.
    Queste sono americane.
    Questo è nuovo.
    Questa è bella.
    Quelli sono belli.
    Quello abita in Italia.
    Quelli sono bravi.
    Quelle sono sporche.
    Quello è molto buono.
89. Dove sono i tuoi?
    Il loro è verde.
    Chi ha le mie?
    La nostra abita in Italia.
    Il suo è simpatico.
90. Chi abita a Roma?
91. Di chi è questo portafoglio?
92. Come ti chiami? (Come si chiama?—polite)
93. Dove abiti (abita)?
94. Quando sei/è andato in Italia?
95. Perché mangia (pol) OR mangi (fam) i dolci?
96. (*see* §7.3–1)
    . . . io sono andato . . . lei ha portato . . . noi due . . .
    Anche loro . . . proprio voi . . . siamo noi . . . Io sono qui
    . . . e tu . . . anche io
97–114 (*see* §7.3–2)
97. Giovanni gli telefonerà domani.
98. Ti penso spesso.
99. Maria mi ha chiamato(-a).

100. Lo chiamerò domani.
101. Tu gli telefonerai.
102. Maria la chiamerà.
103. E poi le telefonerà.
104. Maria ci ha visto(-i) ieri.
105. Il professore vi parlerà.
106. L'ha già data a quel ragazzo.
     Le ha già dato la penna.
     Ieri lo abbiamo mangiato.
     Ieri gli abbiamo telefonato.
     Giovanni me le ha date.
     Mio padre glieli ha mandati.
     Il commesso ce l'ha detta.
     No, non gliele ho date.
     Sì, gliela ha mandata.
107. Sì ti ho chiamato (ieri).
108. No, non mi hanno telefonato.
109. Sì, l'ho ricevuta.
110. No, non te lo darò.
111. Sì, ve la scriverò.
112. Gliele ho già scritte./Gliele ho scritte già.
113. Ve le mando domani./Domani ve le mando.
114. Te li ho dati ieri./Ieri te li ho dati.
115. (*see* §7.4)
     . . . che ho comprato . . . dal quale . . . che il verde . . .
     a cui . . . Quello (Quel, Ciò) che mi piace . . .
116–120 (*see* §7.5)
116. Non si dicono queste cose!
117. Quanta ne hai mangiata?
118. Ci andremo fra due mesi.
119. Non si è mai contenti!
120. Ci sono andati, e poi ne sono tornati.

8.
Verbs

121–123 (*see* §8.2–1 through 8.2–7)
121. eri uscito già
     hai comprato
     andavano
     avranno mangiato
     Costerà
     cominciammo
     paghi
122. mangi
     comincerò
     sono arrivati
     avrà finito
     capì
     scriveva
     metti/hai messo

123. Io non aspetto.
     Tu capisci.
     Lui è uscito.
     Lei è uscita.
     Noi paghiamo il conto.
     Voi parlate troppo.
     Loro finiscono la lezione.

124. (*see* §8.3)
     Signor Santini, lo prenda!
     Marco, scrivila!
     Signorina, me li dia!
     Gino, non parlare!
     Ragazzi, andateci!

125. (*see* §8.4–1 and §8.4–2)
     scriverei
     avrei scritto
     avrebbe mangiato
     mangerebbe

126. (*see* §8.5–1 through 8.5–4)
     arriverà
     finisca
     abbia piovuto
     lavorerai
     potesse
     avessimo conosciuto

127. (*see* §8.7)
     siamo divertiti
     ti alzi
     si ricorda
     vi siete divertite
     me la sono lavata
     alzati
     si metta

128. (*see* §8.6–1, §8.6–2, and 8.9, and review whole
     chapter)
     . . . scrivo . . . sono stato . . . sia stata . . .
     a comprare . . . stavo guardando . . . è venuto . . .
     Voleva . . . avevo . . . ha cominciato . . . ha parlato . . .
     andasse . . . aver parlato . . . decise di andare . . .
     saremo . . . darò . . . amo.

129. (see Verb Charts section of this book)

t	u	i	u	h	n	b	e	v	u	t	o	c	i	o
d	c	l	e	t	t	o	m	e	s	s	o	h	s	n
e	p	h	p	r	e	s	o	d	e	c	t	i	u	a
t	r	r	i	t	t	u	t	i	o	r	t	e	o	t
t	e	i	h	u	u	i	t	b	m	i	n	s	p	o
o	s	g	h	t	s	o	a	h	u	t	k	t	t	o
e	s	t	a	t	o	o	f	o	o	t	o	o	t	o
c	h	i	e	d	s	c	e	l	t	o	d	i	t	t

130. (see §8.8)

La torta è stata mangiata da Giovanni.
Molti regali saranno comprati dai turisti.
Quel libro è letto da tutti.
Credo che quel film sia stato interpretato da Sofia Loren.

9. ADVERBS

131, 132 (see §9.2)
131. raramente, certamente, precisamente, veramente, nuovamente
132. elegantemente, felicemente, regolarmente, difficilmente, popolarmente, benevolmente, leggermente
133–138 (see §9.3)
133. già
134. invece
135. ancora
136. poi
137. spesso, quasi
138. . . . molta fame . . . mangiato molto . . . molto buoni . . . molto buona . . . molte persone . . . molte verdure . . . molta carne
139–142 (see §9.4)
139. migliore
140. meglio
141. miglior(e)
142. meglio

10. PREPOSITIONS

143–148 (see §10.2)
143. nel
     sul
     agli
     dello
     dall'
     nella

144. Sono i libri degli amici di Carla.
145. Ieri siamo andati ai negozi di abbigliamento.
146. Sono negli zaini.
147. Dalle uscite potrete vedere le macchine.
148. Abbiamo dato le tue matite alle ragazze.
149. (*see* §10.3)
... da tre anni ... tra due anni ... in Francia ... per studiare ... a Parigi

**11.
NEGATIVES
AND OTHER
GRAMMAT-
ICAL POINTS**

150. (*see* §11.2)
mai
nessuno
neanche
né ... né
più
niente
mica
151–157 (*see* §11.3)
151. Ecco
152. c'è
153. Qual è
154. sono ... ci sono
155. La madre ha fatto scrivere una cartolina agli zii.
156. Gliela farò comprare
157. Maria non ha fatto lavare i piatti a suo fratello.

**12.
THE VERB
"PIACERE"**

158–162 (*see* §12.2)
158. Sì, mi piace molto.
159. Sì, mi piace e io piaccio a lei (or io le piaccio).
160. Mi piacciono, ma io non piaccio a loro (ma io non gli piaccio).
161. No, non mi è piaciuta, e agli altri non è piaciuta.
162. Sì, mi piaci. (E io) ti piaccio? Ci piacciamo, veramente?
163–166 (*see* §12.3)
163. Sì, mi piace la tua cravatta, ma non mi piacciono i tuoi pantaloni.
164. Ci piacciono i tortellini, ma purtroppo non ci piace il sugo.
165. Ti piace la minestra? A me non piace, ma mi piacciono i ravioli.
166. A lui piace l'italiano, a me piacciono gli sport, a te piace il cinema, a tutti noi non piacciono le barzellette.

**13.
IDIOMATIC
EXPRESSIONS**

167–172 (*see* §13.2)
167. Giovanni ed io abbiamo fame e sete.
168. D'estate loro hanno sempre caldo, ma d'inverno hanno sempre freddo.

169. Signora, Lei ha ragione; io, invece, ho torto.
170. Giovanni, non devi avere vergogna, e non devi avere paura.
171. Ho voglia di andare ad un ristorante stasera.
172. Abbiamo bisogno di due cose quando andremo in centro.
173–176 (*see* §13.3)
173. fare
174. dia . . . sta
175. Faccia . . . fare . . . fa
176. fa . . . fa . . . dà
177. (*see* §13.4)

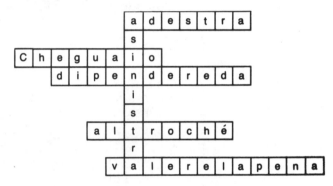

14. NUMBERS

178. (*see* §14.2)
sette, nove, undici, ventuno, quarantadue, cinquantotto, ottantotto, cento ventitré, novecento ottantasette, mille trecento quarantacinque, settantasei mila novecento ottanta, ottocento ottantotto mila ottocento ottantotto, due milioni trecento quarantacinque mila seicento settantotto

179. (*see* §14.3)
(la) quarta ragazza, (le) sedicesime lezioni, (il) ventitreesimo sbaglio, (il) duecento quarantottesimo giorno, (la) quattro mila cinquecento settantottesima pagina

180. (*see* §14.3)
due terzi, un ventottesimo, tre quarti, quindici sedicesimi, trentaquattro ottantanovesimi

181. Maria ha sette anni.
Marco ha dieci anni e Gino ha dodici anni.
Stefano è il più basso.

15. TELLING TIME

182. (*see* §15.2–15.4)
È l'una. Sono le quattro e trenta (mezzo). Sono le due e venti. Sono le sei meno cinque (le cinque e cinquanta).

Sono le quattro e quaranta (le cinque meno venti). Sono le nove meno venti (le otto e quaranta). Sono le sette e quindici (un quarto). Sono le otto e quindici (un quarto).

Sono le venti e trentacinque (le ventuno meno venticinque). Sono le diciannove e trenta (mezzo). Sono le diciotto e quindici (un quarto). Sono le venti e cinque.

Sono le tredici e cinque. Sono le sedici meno venti (le quindici e quaranta). Sono le ventitrè e venticinque. Sono le ventidue e venticinque.

183. (*see* §16.2)

b	ì	s	t	g	i	o	v	e	d	ì
q	r	y	p	m	e	l	e	w	c	k
a	x	v	o	n	i	z	n	u	d	y
p	n	m	a	b	o	v	e	n	l	r
t	h	a	s	o	l	k	r	t	l	o
m	e	r	c	o	l	e	d	ì	s	a
x	c	t	e	j	u	g	ì	h	a	r
v	w	e	t	o	n	i	k	a	b	l
j	u	d	o	m	e	n	i	c	a	x
p	h	i	r	e	d	a	s	o	t	g
z	k	a	y	n	ì	n	o	b	o	r

184. (*see* §16.3)
ottobre
luglio
agosto
dicembre
settembre
novembre
gennaio
giugno
febbraio
maggio
aprile
marzo

185. (*see* §16.4 and §16.5)
primavera
inverno
scorsa
prossimo
fa
A

186. (*see* §16.6)
lunedì, (il) dodici maggio
martedì, (il) venticinque gennaio
mercoledì, (il) primo febbraio
sabato, (il) tre dicembre

187. (*see* §16.7)

tira vento	tuona e lampeggia	piove
fa molto caldo	fa bel tempo	fa freddo

17. COMMON DISCOURSE STRATEGIES

188, 189 (*see* §17.2)

188. Come va?
Non c'è male, grazie, e Lei?
Buon giorno.

189. Chi parla?
Sono Gino. C'è tua sorella?
Arrivederci.

190. (*see* §17.3 and §17.4)
Buona sera, professore.
Come Si chiama?
Mi chiamo Daniela Berti. . . . permette che Le presenti
. . . Le presento Dina Armando.
Piacere . . . conoscenza

191–194 (*see* §17.5)

191. Che noia!

192. Mi dispiace.

193. Non sono d'accordo.

194. Come?

18. SYNONYMS AND ANTONYMS

195, 196 (*see* §18.2)

195. ora—adesso
abito—vestito
vicino—presso
faccia—viso
volentieri—con piacere
quindi—dunque
pazzo—matto
chiedere—domandare

196. ho conosciuto

19.
COGNATES: GOOD AND FALSE FRIENDS

197. piccolo—grande
     magro—grasso
     dentro—fuori
     aperto—chiuso
     pulito—sporco
     alba—tramonto
     chiaro—scuro
     atterraggio—decollo
     presto—tardi

198. (*see* §19.2)

(la) condizione	(la) situazione
(la) conclusione	la società
(l') importanza	(l')attore
(il) vocabolario	(il/la) violinista
(l') oculista	(la) biologia
(la) geologia	tipico
sociale	perfetto
(l') effetto	(l') intelletto

199, 200 (*see* §19.3)

199. la libreria: Il negozio dove si comprano i libri.
     il parente: lo zio, la zia, il cugino . . .
     la fattoria: la casa "in campagna"
     la stampa: si "legge"

200. assisterò
     un incidente
     direttore
     quella rivista
     una ditta grande

Index

The items in this index refer to topics in the *"Brush Up"* part of the book *(Basics, Parts of Speech, Special Topics)*. The symbol § refers to the section of a chapter in which you will find the designated topic (e.g., §10.1 = section 10.1 of the tenth chapter). Page numbers are indicated by *p.* (e.g., *p.* 10), and *ff* stands for "following" (e.g., *p.* 10 *ff* = page 10 and following).

229

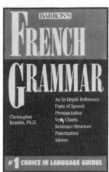